The
Ape
in
Me

The Ape in Me

by Cornelia Otis Skinner

with drawings by alaJálov

HOUGHTON MIFFLIN COMPANY BOSTON

THE RIVERSIDE PRESS CAMBRIDGE

Contents

The
Ape
in
Me

...if it is true that we have sprung from the ape...

The Ape
in Me

When I was in boarding school we had an English teacher who had a slight but habitual twitch to her nose. It was not in the least a detracting mannerism, being almost imperceptible and the teacher herself being pretty and charming. I admired her fatuously and wanted to be just like her . . . a forlorn ambition, for she was curly-blond, blue-eyed and rosy while I was dark-eyed, stringy-haired and sallow. My

only resemblance to her . . . and at that an un-
intentional one . . . was in regard to that nose
twitch. The nervous little habit would become a
fascinating distraction from the dedicated study
of literature. If I watched her for long, my own
nose would start doing an involuntary act in
imitation of hers. The more self-conscious I
became about it, the more it would intensify
until toward the end of class, to my deep em-
barrassment, I'd be matching her twitch for
twitch like an eager Peter Rabbit.

I would long since have dismissed such com-
pulsive mimicry as a manifestation of adolescent
nonsense, but then some years ago there married into our family an attractive younger man
("younger" with me these days means anywhere
between thirty-five and forty-five). His attractions
are enhanced by the presence of an engaging tic
in his left eye which causes him to wink at un-
expected moments. When I first met him, I
was under the pleased impression that he was
winking at me in a manner I hoped was insin-
uating of all sorts of things. I didn't wink back,
partly because I was afraid it would look too
brash, partly because it is practically impossible
for me to deliberately lower one eyelid without
closing down both at the same time. And when it

comes to innuendo, a blink could never give the
effect of a wink. It wasn't long before I regret-
fully discovered that what I had taken as a subtle bid for my favors was no more than a muscular
spasm. Too bad! What makes it worse is that
now, when I get into any lengthy conversation
with him, *my* eye starts having a few spasms
of its own and there we are, giddily winking
away at each other even if the subject under
discussion is as unwinking a matter as the foreign situation or the imminent demise of crazy
old Cousin Harriet. If this attractive younger
man notices such seemingly forward behavior
on my part, he is gentlemanly enough not to
take it as a come-on signal. Which, come to
think of it, is too bad also.

It is disturbing to discover in oneself these
curious revelations of the validity of the Dar-
winian theory. If it is true that we have sprung
from the ape, there are occasions when my own
spring appears not to have been very far. When
I go to the theatre . . . and I go frequently
. . . I am told that if a play is especially absorbing, I express my interest by making a series
of faces which are exact reproductions of the
expressions of the players up on the stage. If
a performer exhibits astonishment, my eyebrows

go up and my mouth opens in reciprocal response. If it's glee, I leer; if pathos, I take on the wistfulness of a Gish in *Orphans of the Storm*. If a scene is heartrending, I look like a Greek mask of tragedy, which is a pretty terrible way to look, and when love dawns . . . well, I'd just as soon not search for a simile. It is fortunate that the darkness of the auditorium cloaks these shifting grimaces, for I have no idea when I am making them. Actually I would never have known that I did if it hadn't been for one evening when attending an unusually tense drama, I began to realize that the gentleman friend who had brought me there was staring intently not at the star of the performance but at me. I whispered to him, "Just watch that actor's facial expressions." "I am," he whispered back, "on you. I've been watching you make them for the past ten minutes!" I croaked a meek "Oh" and sat through the remainder of the show rigidly trying to control my face, which for me at the theatre is obviously as impossible as for a jazz aficionado to control his beating foot at a hot jam session.

In addition to my copying-actors'-face, or faces, there is my watching-other-people-eat imitation. It makes me feel less of an oddity to realize that in this eccentricity I am not unique. Quite a few people go through interesting facial contortions while watching others consume food. Take, for example, the average mother performing the duties of spoon-feeding the average baby. She will hold up the porridge dish replete with milk, Pablum and dietetic whatnot and start stirring with starry-eyed enthusiasm, her lips going through yum-yum motions if not indeed doing a bit of delicate, anticipatory drooling. Then she will scoop out a spoonful and approach it to baby's rosebud mouth, at the same time her own full-blown aperture gaping wide like the beak of a nestling robin, and as she plops home as much of the pretty gunk as does not ooze out and on down the dimpled chin, she will enact a complete pantomime of savoring, chewing, swallowing and general ecstasizing. It has been years since I went through the darling process, but I daresay that I too put on a similar divertissement, mouthing in imagination the gooey snacks which I forcibly fed to my son and which he almost instantly returned. Even at this much later date, my offspring complains of my table mimicry. He says that at the moment when he or his father are about to try a first taste of some new and special dish, they are put off by what he calls my expression of an expectant carp at feeding time and are further annoyed to see my jaws open, close and chew in exact synchronization with theirs, even if there's nothing in my own mouth.

The unconscious antics of the hidden ape in me are not limited to facial mimicry. There are peculiarities of gesture which I take on as a chameleon takes on color. That, parenthetically, is an erroneous comparison, for every chameleon I was ever given as a child or purchased as a mother for my own child was either color-blind or plain stubborn and no matter how bright the hue it was placed upon, always remained a bilious green. I do, however, take on gestures, particularly those of foreigners, and of the foreigners I really go to town over Latins. Get me together with a Frenchman (and I dearly like being got together with many Frenchmen) and I'll outmatch him shrug for shrug. Even in a Gallic telephone booth, I have all but to step outside for the wider range of my gesticulating free arm. As for Italians, the exuberant sort who talk as much with their hands as with their tongues, I can best illustrate my imitative response by recalling an evening in Naples when after a spirited discussion of the menu with a head waiter my husband observed, "For a while there

I thought you and that fellow were starting up a game of Pease Porridge Hot."

The European custom of shaking hands on all occasions is something for which I fall with alacrity. It began when I was a student in Paris and living with a French family. We shook hands when we said good morning, we shook hands when we said good night and we shook hands when we met for meals. I was more than once tempted to spy through the keyhole of Monsieur and Madame's bedroom to find out if when they waked, they started the day by sitting up in bed and cordially shaking hands with each other. The formality still takes hold and when I return to the States, it's only the fear of over-doing things which restrains me from shaking hands with the customs inspector.

And speaking of handshaking, there is the manner in which certain persons shake mine which is precisely the manner in which I shake theirs back. If I meet up, with a vigorous hand-shaker, my response is so co-operatively vigorous, we both say "Ouch." If it's a question of the limp-handed, I hold forth a wilting and dislo-cated paw. There is a type of overblown and over-exuberant matron who plows backstage after a matinee and who has a horrifying way of grabbing one's hand, plonking it flat against her upholstered bosom and holding it there for excruciating minutes. I have yet to respond with kindred action, but I live in dread that I might.

Such are only a few of the imitative failings of a supine nature. Take accents, for instance. And that's exactly what I do . . . I take on every variety, blithely, shamelessly and unconsciously. After a few days in England or, for that matter, after a mere few hours on a British liner, I begin talking in the strangulated diction of the Londoner who, when asked if he were English, sputtered apoplectically, "By Jove, old chap, if I were any *more* English, I shouldn't be able to speak at all!" I have never known the delights of a visit to Scotland, but I'm awfully afraid that I'd clamber about Stirling Castle doing a ham impersonation of Flora MacDonald. I have, however, been to Ireland, playing a theatrical engagement in Dublin, a city with which I fell passionately in love. I had not realized to what extremes the passion had gone until my husband, who now and then exerts a healthily subduing influence over my enthusiasms, upon hearing me exchange some top-o'-the-mornin' chit-chat with the Shelbourne Hotel porter asked what the hell did I think

I was doing, practicing for an audition at the Abbey Theatre?

At home in America, this mockingbird compulsion is just as bad. Mine is a profession which entails frequent and extensive touring. Sometimes my schedule will keep me for a prolonged stopover in a state where if the native sons talk with a special regional accent, it doesn't take long for me to become a native daughter as far as *my* accent goes. And it goes right off at every geographical tangent. Give me a month in the Middle West (only please specify where in the Middle West before you give it to me) and my *r*'s commence rolling like equipment in a Gary steel works — grinding out that earsplitting consonant which my father once designated as "The Great American *r* which gathers force as it roars across the midwestern plains until it shatters on the Rockies." If, on the other hand, I tarry amid the tidy houses and immemorial elms or New England, my *r*'s are deleted in an academic pronunciation as clipped as the grass on a municipal green. I might be getting into the mood for a public reading of "The Courtship of Miles Standish." A *park* is a *pack,* a *barn* is a *ban* and while I can't quite believe that I substitute *aye-ah* for my customary melodious *yeah,* it's not beyond the realms of possibility. Then there is the South. I happen to be one of those old Northern sourpusses who does not go into lyrical ecstasies over every Southern accent. Certain ones, to be sure, are soft and engaging while others are shrill and distressing. And there are still others which strike me as being just plain silly, spoken by the type of Dixiecrat who gives the impression of flaunting the exaggerated dialect because it's impractical to carry around a Confederate flag on all occasions. It comes as a shock, therefore, to discover that this last is the one I adopt as I hear myself coming out with a drawl that's all magnolias, hush-puppies and whippoorwills. When I run across acquaintances, instead of a well-bred "How nice to see you!" or even a matey "Hello there," I lilt a languid "Hi!" pronouncing it "Ha!" and assure them-all that Ah'm mahghty glaid to see them-all this evenin' (*evenin'* bein' . . . woops! *being* any hour from one minute past noon on). As for that gory and tragic conflict between the States which this side of the Mason-Dixon is called the Civil War and down there is known simply as "The Wa-wa," like any tactful Yankee I try to avoid mention of it, as Southerners have a polite but inexorable way of making me feel personally

responsible for Sherman's March to the Sea. In
the more historic states, however, the subject is
bound to come up, in which delicate situation I
speak with cautious respect of "The Waugh" as
in Evelyn. Apparently this tendency to slip into
the lingo of the Little Colonel is not necessarily
dependent upon a setting of white pillars and
Spanish moss. A good friend from Mississippi
whom I've not seen in years arrived in town the
other day and called me up. I was so delighted to
hear again her cheery "Honey chile, hah yu?"
I answered with the response of an end man in a
minstrel show, "Sugah, Ah'm fahn, hah yu?"

Then there are any number of individuals with
tricks of pronunciation which without my knowing it will creep into my own. My nearest and
dearest friend hails from Indiana. It has been
some time since she hailed, but her parlance is
still colored by an endearing Hoosierism or two.
In place of the adverb "later" she uses "after-
ward," which would not seem too odd if she didn't
pronounce it "afterWURRD." It seemed still
odder not long ago when she asked if I'd care for
a bite before going to a movie we'd planned to
take in, to hear myself saying "No, let's eat
afterWURRD." Another friend has taken up
the smart-set fad of inserting the word *but* for

emphasis before an adjective. To her a good play is *"but* terrific," an indifferent novel *"but* dismal," Upper-U slang which I find asinine, and knowing the lady well I told her as much. My words might have carried some weight if I hadn't summed them up with "What's more, it's *but* ungrammatical!"

There is yet another woman I know who talks with the too-too-divine Park Avenue lockjaw. She sounds almost like a take-off of herself and, what's more she uses a broad *a* on everything. A *man* is a *mahn,* a couple might walk "hond in hond," England's royal race track is *Oscot* while even the simple conjunctive *and* is fancied up to rhyme with "pond" . . . all quite idiotic and yet when she happened to mention a rather distasteful crooner recently, I came out with a forthright "There's someone I cannot *stond."*

In addition to pronunciation there are tones of voice. With someone who talks exceptionally softly, I subdue my speech to the degree that anybody hearing us, or rather *not* hearing us, would think that either we were exchanging secrets or were about to step into the next room and view the remains. While by contrast there are those who go on an assumption that everyone else is deaf and to them I halloo back as though they were the deafest of all. This brings me to the old cliché about meeting up with a stammerer and coming down with a stammer oneself. Which is quite true, and with me it's even more so, for I happen at times to have a slight stammer. It is not habitual, but it will suddenly hit me now and then on such occasions as when I might be telling my family a long and involved anecdote and all of a sudden realize that they are paying me strict attention . . . a situation so unusual, it stops me dead and I become inarticulate. Expose me to a severe stammerer and things become very awful indeed as communication between us becomes virtually impossible. I usually walk away as soon as courtesy will permit. It seems kinder than launching into what gives every indication of being a heartless take-off.

I daresay that if I were to make further study of my apelike behavior, I should also discover that I copy the way other people walk. But my discoveries to date are depressing enough, being obvious indications of a weak and unoriginal character. The solacing day will be when I become happily aware that someone is imitating ME!

. . . an ice pick and a stream of profanity . . .

Press Here
to Open

I have usually looked upon myself . . . that is when I am obliged to do so . . . as a good tempered, *laissez-faire* individual who, if not the female counterpart of Abou Ben Adhem when it came to loving my fellow man, at least hated none of them. None, that is, whom I knew or could identify. There is, to be sure, one exception in a person on whom I have come to vent all the hatred, spleen and venom of an otherwise benevolent nature, and that is whoever invented the zipper. Not a week has gone by since the nasty gadget invaded our daily life but what I have fervently repeated an elaborate curse which dooms its inventor upon his demise to go directly to hell, there for his body to be encased in a garment, tight-fitting and bessemer-hot, removable only by means of one of his own zippers which runs up and down the back and is eternally getting jammed at a halfway point of no recovery.

Lately, however, I discover to my alarm that my capacity for hatred is increasing. The sadist who cursed civilization with the zipper is no longer the sole recipient of my venom; it is being expended daily upon those wretched unknowns who are responsible for American packaging . . . those wizards of cardboard, waxed paper, cellophane, Scotch tape, red tabs saying "Pull," red dots saying "Push," semi-perforated hyphen lines saying "Open Here" and further easy steps to madness, who are responsible for causing our consumer goods to reach us in boxes, containers, wrappers and cartons that are not only increasingly hideous, but increasingly unopenable. What seems preposterous is the childish self-congratulation with which the various industries launch each new bundling device with publicity hosannas to the effect that here is that dear old product you've been buying for years, but now it comes to you in brand-new, up-to-date covering which is one more triumph of American packaging. If the dear old product has survived the years, why couldn't its dear old wrappings remain the same?

Even the department stores are falling in with the deplorable trend and simple purchases tend more and more to arrive done up in ways that are not only uninviting but bafflingly complicated.

I am especially aware of this, having recently visited Japan where the wrapping up of everything from a rare vase to a package of soy beans is a minor work of art and one more charming amenity to life in that graceful land. Order something to be delivered from one of Tokyo's leading stores and it arrives in a pretty box, covered in attractive paper and festively tied with ribbon or colored string, as inviting as a Christmas present . . . and what's more, an easy-to-open Christmas present. Order something from one of our large emporia and it is likely as not to arrive in a dreary brown box, covered in dreary brown paper, hermetically sealed with unappetizing tape and marked "Fragile." All the good clean fun of opening a parcel seems to me to be going out of American life . . . It is now a complicated chore (unless I except my own Christmas parcels which my friends and relatives inform me have a generous way of opening themselves in the mails). There used to be a happy expectancy attendant to undoing a shop delivery, even if one knew perfectly well that all it contained was a pair of newly soled shoes. As for those interesting fanatics whose peculiar passion was the careful undoing and saving of string and twine, the poor creatures must be reduced to the dismal extremity of having to buy it. The present bent is "utilitarian," we are told. Well, perhaps it is, in a way, for quite a number of implements are utilized with which to attempt to pry, rip or wrench open the covering to some object which in the first place needed no more elaborate protection than what would be sufficient for transporting a dozen dish towels.

Not long ago my husband made a few purchases in a sporting goods shop which shall remain incognito other than to hint that it has two names of which the second rhymes with "bitch." The purchases were delivered with smart promptitude. They had been packed in a cardboard box which was both stiff and enormous. It was stoutly taped with a blond version of the sort of sticky adhesive they bind about the handles of tennis racquets. Not only were the sides where the top cover fits down over the lower one so taped, all six of the remaining edges were similarly bound and bandaged. It must have been due to some overwhelming sense of symmetry on the part of the packager, or perhaps he harbored a secret loathing for all customers and found perverse satisfaction in thinking of their bafflement in trying to figure out a point at which to start wedging the thing apart. The cardboard was as sturdy as plywood and the tape as unyielding as cement. After the tip flew off the library scissors, it took my largest carving knife, a can opener, an ice pick and a stream of profanity to reach the carefully guarded "Fragile" contents which consisted of two flannel shirts, one cashmere muffler and three pairs of woolen socks. A hole jabbed by the ice pick through the bosom of one of the shirts remains as an honorable scar of the fray.

Such elaborate bundling of the unbreakable is by no means limited to dry goods. What strikes me as fantastic as it is senseless is the number of indignities perpetrated upon books. For generations a book used to be sent by shop or publisher simply and properly done up in a piece of heavy paper, twine and at the most a layer of corrugated carton. It never failed to arrive intact, looking tidy and inviting. What has got into the brains of bookdealers lately that they now send out books in encasings which would be just the ticket for the shipping of Venetian glass? Even a paperback comes in a hideous envelope so heavily padded it might in an emergency serve as a tea cozy. It has one supposedly open end. At least the words "Open Here" run along a certain portion which is not only glued together, it has been further occluded by some hateful little metal clamps so firmly embedded, they appear to have been welded on. To pry it asunder is next to impossible. What one usually pries off is a jagged hole in the outer layer of the envelope and what comes forth is not the book but the inner wadding in a gray snowstorm of dingy pulp flakes like the stuffing used for the insulation of houses. It flies all over carpet and clothes and the pleasures of inspecting the book have to await the ministrations of whiskbroom and vacuum cleaner.

A further outrage perpetrated by the shippers

of books is when, being apparently stingy with postage, they send the bill along with it — only, instead of enclosing it inside the volume in a convenient and human fashion, they place it in an envelope addressed to the customer and then affixed to the outside with a passepartout framework of Scotch tape. I have failed to renew my subscription to a rather highbrow book club because each month both book and bill were expedited in this infuriating fashion. Freeing the envelope containing the bill from its soldering of Scotch tape meant a general mangling that reduced the whole thing into virtual illegibility. Well, now that I come to think about it, maybe I was not the one who failed to renew the subscription.

Put me down as an old fuddy — who still prays for the return of the horse and buggy — but I admit to being one of that stuffy minority who fail to offer up daily prayers of gratitude for the unmitigated blessing of cellophane. I find the blessing extremely mitigated, not infrequently to the degree of becoming a curse. There is no computing the vast number of products, commodities, market goods and what may as well be called "things" that come sealed, signed, delivered and mummified in the exasperating stuff. Many of these articles bear on the outside of their gleaming and sterile cocoon a smug little notice which reads "For your protection." Not only is this statement pontifically smug, it is outrageously misleading, for what is protected is not *you,* but the article imprisoned within the cellophane which is often so protected as to be wellnigh ungetatable. For the average cellophane encasing is a little demonstration in the theory of eternity. It has no beginning and no end. Sometimes there is a small gesture of consideration for the consumer by way of a red tab and the instruction "Pull." Obediently you pull and what happens? You quickly and neatly pull off the red tab and the cellophane remains intact, still in its eternity state of no beginning and no end. The cigarette pack is of course the obvious example of this annoyance. But there are countless other similarly packaged annoyances. For instance, salted peanuts. And if you're not a salted-peanut eater, how do you like sitting in a train or movie house in front of an addict who in the crackling efforts to get at the contents of the bag borders on the limits of becoming a public nuisance! And for further example there are those tidy little envelopes of tasty after-dinner mints with which the airline passenger is invited to top off his sky-high meal. Next time you have this interesting opportunity, just observe a passenger in the throes of attempting to release three small white peppermints from their cellophane confinement. He will rumple the edge of the bag, tear at it, try ripping it with a fingernail, even snap at it with an eyetooth and finally wind up gouging both it and the cushion of his thumb with the prong of a fork.

The purpose of cellophane, obviously, is to keep commodities in a state of pristine sterility and consequently, like all things sterile, the commodities immediately lose all character. Vegetables exhibited in cellophane bags look tasteless and as though they had never known any contact with the earth. Who minds a little healthy dirt . . . or a few healthy germs, for that matter? The best bread in the world is in France where a baker would no more desecrate a delicious, crusty loaf by encasing it in the idiotic stuff than a Côte d'Or vintner would serve wine in a waxed paper cup.

Greater and more absurd packaging is slowly taking over our markets and grocery stores. Containers are becoming more and more objects that merely contain and refuse to let go. I have had more in sorrow than in anger to change the brand of beer I've enjoyed for years. It is now being put out in a fancy new carton from which, the brewers point out with pride, the cans can't possibly fall out. This is so true. They cannot possibly fall out, or be worked or wrenched out unless one rips the carton more or less into shreds and when that exhausting task is accomplished, all six cans bound out at once, topple onto the linoleum and roll under the stove. During the summer months we live in the country where we get our eggs from a local poultry lady. She puts them up in square, sensible old-fashioned egg boxes each marked "Eggs" and embellished with the picture of a well-satisfied hen who looks to have just laid the whole dozen. These boxes are simplicity itself to handle and no egg has ever been known to break in transit in my car unless some unwary passenger in the back seat has had the bad judgment to sit down on a box. The eggs *I* get from my city grocer don't break in transit either. When they do break is if I pull too hard in trying to extract one from its private cell in the up-to-date egg container, an elaborate job dreamed up by some packaging expert who must have harbored a lifelong hatred for eggs. It is all wedges and cardboard cutouts as intricate as the wooden slivers of a Chinese puzzle. Tug too vigorously on one of the imprisoned eggs and the shell quite understandably shatters. It also remains imprisoned. And it emits an overflow of horrid goo that would be fine for tempera painting but isn't so fine for the adjacent eggs, especially after it hardens and shellacs them into further captivity.

The household commodities now presented in modern packaging are too numerous to list. However, by way of diversion, I should like to mention two time-honored staples which might profit by a little up-to-date covering, for they have always reached the consumer in unopenable form. One is . . . are . . . sardines. Maybe there exist somewhere a few deft geniuses who can manipulate a tin of sardines. Maybe they can effortlessly free that key which is soldered onto the lid and then twist off the narrow metal strip without its getting all fouled up and running free of the key. And maybe they don't eventually have to resort to a can opener and a jabbing operation which results in a mincing of the sardines and a fish-oil bath for the hands. The other household commodity which could do with a little simplification is shoe polish, the sort put out in a little round tin box to open which, say the encircling instructions, one need only "insert a coin." What coin, they tactfully fail to specify. The last time I tried to split apart one of these maddening little contraptions, I happened to be clad solely in a nylon nightgown, a costume with which I don't usually carry around coins. It meant going downstairs for my bag, ferreting out the coin purse and finding it contained four pennies, two dimes and a silver dollar good luck piece. I tried inserting the penny, that is, I tried to find some semblance of a crack into which to slip the penny. The coin and my fingers merely shot round and round the box in giddy circles. Thinking that maybe a penny might be too stingy, I tried a dime, but with similarly futile results. The silver dollar I knew could hardly be inserted into anything short of a Nevada slot machine. I then tried a letter opener which will open letters no more, and a nail file whose tip also snapped off. I hammered the box with the heel of the shoe I wanted to polish, I whacked it with a poker. The stubborn little object remained as tightly closed as the two halves of a vacuum sphere. Finally with an access of strength heightened by the adrenalin of fury, I hurled it against the wall.

And that, kind reader, is the best way in which to open a tin of shoe polish. It is also a pretty good way in which to nick a chunk of plaster out of your wall, but what do you care as long as you get at the polish?

One might go on ad infinitum. Even in the pharmaceutical world there are any number of odd innovations of the "press here," "slide there" or "turn to open" sort in addition to weird "improvements" such as plastic bottle-top covers that look like miniature space helmets and require almost the use of a small handsaw to remove. (Incidentally what ever happened to all those nice little old medicine bottles gracefully stoppered with a nice little old cork . . . like Castoria or Stoke's Expectorant or somebody else's Emulsion? For that matter, what ever happened to corks?) Take the small "pocket size" tin box of aspirin . . . that is, if you're suffering from a cold . . . It used to be quite easy to open. Now it's even easier or so we are led to believe by the persons who have overhauled the humble tin receptacle and embellished it with certain jack-in-the-box properties. Now instead of just opening the thing in a fashion known to man since the days when man invented boxes one must bear down thumb and forefinger pressure onto either a red dot or an indented corner (according to the brand of aspirin one prefers) thereby releasing not only the lid but the tablets which immediately fly forth like quail out of a covey, and one is left with a small tin box denuded of its contents except for a folded bit of literature which, it is to be surmised, extolls the charms and merits of aspirin, although I have never found spare time in which to read the fascinating tract. Then there is the sort of bottle (I am thinking specifically of my own throat gargle) whose thin metal top splits neatly apart if twisted in a certain manner. A few gouge marks in the woodwork of my bathroom doorjamb bear testimony of how efficacious my manner must have been.

What to me is almost more distressing than having to deal with all these super-duper packaged articles is the docility with which we the public not only accept them but fool ourselves into thinking many of them are "cute." I recently ran across one such whimsy in a hotel where I had ordered a breakfast, an item of which was a portion of cereal of the flake variety. The flakes were served in their original single-helping box which was illustrated with the usual bright and cheery literature and illustration (why is breakfast considered such a bouncing-with-joy-and-energy meal by the makers of dry cereals?) and the coy instructions that if the happy consumer "pressed" to open along a line of indented hyphen lines, he could fold back the four sections of the top and there lo and behold would be a tidy little dish . . . in other words he could enjoy the delectable novelty of pouring cream and sugar all over the flakes and eating them right out of the container.

Suddenly I was the victim of a hideous vision of a future, packaging-ridden America where endless families living in split-level or ranch-type "homes" sat viewing one another through endless picture windows as they consumed endless meals out of cartons, paper boxes, waxed cups and tin cans. When that era dawns, I shall be quite ready to select my nice snug coffin complete with brass plate on which no doubt will appear the words "Press Here to Open."

...a lot of fun in Capri deflowering maidens...

My Life
with the Punes
on a
Desert Island

I used to think of myself as being a rather well-informed person. That was in the halcyon days before television. It has taken the quiz programs to shatter this fond delusion. I don't really like quiz programs and I quite hate all winning contestants. Not the $64,000 expert who specializes in one single subject, but the bright freak who comes glibly forth with the correct answer on any subject from the exact score of the 1927

World Series to the exact number of grains contained in a family-size box of puffed rice.

Exactitude seems to be the goal of this contest in exhibitionism. I've become particularly aware of this unimaginative angle on "over-all information" in cases where the contestants are asked to answer questions concerning history. I once thought I knew quite a lot about history, but now I wonder. Rather, I wonder how much the prize-winning wise guys know about that colorful subject. What they do know is a raft of dates . . . those distracting and highly irritating footnotes to an otherwise absorbing narrative. To show off one's knowledge of dates is like being asked what the So-and-So's are like and by way of reply, giving their telephone number. Familiarity with an outline of the story of peoples and their times ought to constitute the average layman's cognizance of history and I had conceived myself a cut above the average layman until the quiz program revealed to me that as a historical scholar I'm back in First Grade with Washington just about to chop down the cherry tree and not even thinking about the shores of the Delaware.

This intellectual deficiency is something to brood about. In fact, not long ago, I brooded about it during the better part of a wakeful night.

I started wondering how much history, offhand, I knew. Night thoughts warp the imagination and I found myself building up the terrifying fantasy of myself marooned on a desert island along with a small band of survivors of some shipwreck. We were, I decided, under the able command of a leader . . . a sort of combination of Miles Standish and the Admirable Crichton. There were a few children in our valiant group and the leader felt that their education, even though temporarily interrupted by a stay on the desert island, must be kept up. Accordingly, he appointed certain adults to be instructors in various subjects. What if, I thought, he were to order me to teach history? How would I go about it . . . without textbooks, without an encyclopedia or almanac, without even a battered old novel by Sabatini? What, given these spare circumstances, did I know? I spent the remainder of the night making out the sorry inventory.

Being a dutiful American, I started by reconstructing what I could recall of our country's story and felt confident that I could get away with a few highlights. There would be no dates, of course (how would I be expected to remember dates when I can't remember my own telephone number!), except 1492, 1776 and 1926 which was when Gertrude Ederle swam the English Channel. I doubted if I'd have anything to say about treaties or international policies or economics. So I figured that I could invent a lot of spirited anecdotes about Pilgrim Fathers and Salem Witches and Cavaliers and Quakers; not to forget those famous automotive explorers, Cadillac, La Salle, Chevrolet, De Soto and Pontiac — or was Pontiac an automotive Indian? Then I could explain how Louisiana was opened up by French adventurers who got fed up with adventuring, so the Home Office shipped them out a lot of ladies known as the "filles de casquette" which is polite for prostitute and hence the opera *Manon* as well as the opera *Manon Lescaut*. Then there might be some nice campfire tales such as the killing of Alexander Hamilton by Aaron Burr, and how Barbara Frietchie whooped out at Jackson "Shoot if you must this old gray head" but how Jackson was too much of a Southern gentleman to give way to the temptation to comply. And how Horace Greeley who had a beard growing out of his neck said "Go west, young man" and how the Donner family, who must have taken him overseriously, followed his instruction only to get stuck in the snows of the Sierras where they ended up by eating each other. There could be any number of colorful thumbnail sketches . . . Paul Revere's horse, Mrs. O'Leary's cow, Davy Crockett's coonskin hat. And all those catch phrases which are frightfully historic . . . "No Taxation without Representation," "Bleeding Kansas," "Don't Tread on Me" and "Tippecanoe and Tyler Too" which sounds like a college cheer, and may well be one for all I know of its meaning. Yes, I mused, teaching American history without recourse to textbook might not be an impossible task.

The difficulty would come with the other countries. Where to begin? Back in primitive times with the Neanderthal Man? Not that I could remotely have said where Neanderthal was, nor what the Man was doing in it. There was also the Piltdown Man. But he turned out to be a fake. Anyhow people like them along with Cro-Magnons and Lake Dwellers and Picts and Druids were hardly history. They'd be up to the island anthropologist.

Better begin with early civilizations. Egypt, for instance. What did I know about Egypt other than the fact, once pointed out by Will Cuppy, that the Nile runs the wrong way . . . the Upper Nile being down at the bottom of the map, while the Lower Nile is up at the top? Well, the ruling families were known as dynasties and they had kings called Pharaohs who had names like Imhotp and Amenhotp and other hotps (don't ask me how you pronounce "hotp" . . . the only clue is that Ptolemy is pronounced with a *T* as in Ptennessee). By way of variety there was, I *think,* one king named Cheops, only I wasn't certain whether Cheops was a king or a city. Actually it sounded more like a cut of meat. These Pharaohs who were of a morbid nature were always erecting pyramids as tombs for themselves and, as they were also very conceited, having colossal statues of themselves carved out of rock near Luxor, or Memphis. Or was it Thebes? And why wasn't Thebes in Greece? Maybe it was. And they had a high old time seeing to it that slaves were being constantly flogged, and having their favorite cats mummified and, every now and then, marrying their own sisters or mothers. There was a god named Ra, who owes his posterity to the Cross-Word Puzzle. And naturally there was Cleopatra who had the asp, after she'd had Mark Antony, that is. She also had a Needle, but the Metropolitan Museum seems to have that now. And before Cleopatra there was Tut-ankh-amen, known to his intimates, mostly newspaper men, as "King Tut," who didn't do

anything much except die and leave a cluttered
tomb. Then there were some queens . . . Nefer-
titi who was very beautiful, Hatshepsut who occasionally when the mood struck her dressed as a
man and wore a false beard. She also married her
own brother, but she didn't like him very much.
I'd cut that part about marrying her brother as
a bad moral example for our island colony. I
would also cut King Farouk, because it would be
such fun to cut King Farouk. And there would
be Egypt in a nutshell, or a scarab, if you prefer.

Next, I figured, would have to come Greece
and here I would do nicely with legends from
Greek mythology, even if they hardly counted as
history. I'm awfully up on the Trojan War.
Only that didn't happen in Greece, and indeed
some academic spoilsports would lead us to believe that it never happened at all. This landed
me back on the rugged shores of Attica not knowing where to start or, having started, how to continue. Let's see. There were all those kingdoms,
Ithaca, Thessaly, Athens-the-Cradle-of-Culture,
Sparta full of Spartans who were always doing
idiotic things such as leaving their babies ex-
posed overnight on mountaintops to show just
how Spartan they could be. And there was that
Spartan youth who did the still more idiotic

thing of concealing a fox or a wolf under his
cloak and calmly letting it eat out his insides
without even so much as saying Ouch. The
Athenians didn't get on too well with the Spartans (can you blame them?) and there was a good
deal of internecine warfare known as Pelopon-
nesian (1st and 2nd) and some invasions known as
Persian Wars (1st and 2nd and maybe 3rd). I
could tell about the Pass at Thermopylae, which
would be stirring. And Marathon with that runner, which would be sporting, even if the runner
did fall dead on delivery of his message, or torch
or whatever it was . . . thus making it all part of
the sport. I'd try to speak eloquently of Socrates,
which would be inspiring. And of his death,
which would be sad. And I might dwell lightly
on Pericles, which would be spicy, especially if
I were to bring in a sly reference to Aspasia.
Then there was Diogenes who lived in a tub because he could never find an honest man, and
Archimedes who invented something very important, and Alcibiades who was Greek and very
historical. I would, I supposed, have to make
mention of Alexander the Great and that embarrassing story about his crying because he had no
more worlds to conquer . . . although I hoped
nobody would ask me just which worlds he al-

ready *had* conquered. Other things must have happened in Greece but I don't know just what — so we'd proceed to Rome.

Roman history must always start off with the pretty tale of Romulus and Remus and their milk from contented wolves. Then I'd talk about patriots, orators and triumvirs . . . not naming too many, perhaps, just stating the essential fact that there *were* patriots, like Pyrrhus, and orators like Cato who at the drop of a toga got up and said "Carthage must be destroyed" and triumvirs like . . . well, who cares what a triumvir is anyway? Attention should be paid to the Gracchus boys and their mother, my namesake, who was a Roman Matron and consequently offensively noble (Roman Matrons were as tiresome about being noble as Spartans were about being Spartan). I guessed that I should have to bring up that old enemy of my schooldays, Cicero, along with his oration . . . only I'd not get started on the latter as it took me two terms, the second a repeat, to struggle through that classic filibuster. There would be a few emperors to mention . . . Nero who fiddled, Trajan who put up a column, Hadrian who put up a wall, Augustus who was good, Marcus Aurelius who was even better and Tiberius who was awful, although he did have

a lot of fun in Capri deflowering maidens and
then having them flung from a high cliff so they
wouldn't talk. Rome, like every self-respecting
country, had a lot of wars. There were the Punic
Wars (1st and 2nd). Only what could I say about
the Punic Wars when I have not the slightest idea
who the Punes were? Or did they have something to do with Hannibal? And wasn't there
someone named Hamilcar Barca? There must
have been, for you couldn't just make up a name
like that! Oh well, better go on to Julius Caesar.
Here Shakespeare and Shaw would help jog my
memory. But then Caesar did other things beside placing a crown on his own head (not to be
confused with Napoleon who did the same, but
later) or getting himself assassinated, or dallying
with Cleopatra, whom we have already had.
There were those endless campaigns when he
marched about dividing Gaul into Three Parts,
and pitching his camp across rivers (not to be
confused with George Washington pitching a dollar across the Rappahannock). He was continually coming up against an individual named
Vercingetorix, who sounds like a toothpaste ad-
ditive, and he, like Cicero, was responsible for
an unconscionably tedious textbook, the absence
of which would be one of the blessings of our

island paradise. And that, I decided, disposed of the Roman Empire, except for later when we'd come to the Holy Roman one, which, it has been said, was neither holy nor Roman and it wasn't exactly an empire, so maybe we wouldn't have to come to it at all.

With Caesar and Gaul, we'd advance into Europe and those Ages, known as Dark and Middle. I'm not too well up on the Dark ones except to know that those were times of invasions when Norsemen and Danes and Vikings and things came roaring down the coastal waters in long-boats, drinking out of animal horns and singing like crazy, while inland there were Goths and Visigoths and Ostrogoths and other Goths whom we might as well call Huns for short. But amid all the carnage, fire, ravishing and other silly behavior, there were certain nice heroes like Roland who got caught in a mountain pass and blew his horn but no one answered, a sad situation which inspired a most famous and most unreadable poem called "The Song of Roland" over which French writers are prone to get terribly worked up, although I'll bet not one of them has ever waded through it. So much for the Dark Ages.

The Middle Ages would be easier and more

entertaining, for I still remember Hugo's *Notre Dame* and, given a chance and a few drinks, I'll sing an entire repertory from the *Vagabond King*. There were all those alchemists trying to discover something known as the Philosopher's Stone, and poor little Hugh of Lincoln who got boiled in oil and consequently beatified, and all the tragic young innocents who perished during the Children's Crusade, which always makes me cry. But then by contrast, there were those other fun crusades with gallant knights being energetically gallant, riding around rescuing maidens out of towers, hacking Saracens to mincemeat and getting themselves sung at by troubadours, while their womenfolk stayed home keeping the castle fires burning, doing tapestry needlepoint, tending unicorns and having mad affairs with handsome pageboys. I would, of course, omit all reference to chastity belts.

Then there is always England (and pray God always will be). There was King Arthur and his Round Table, King Alfred and those cakes, Robert Bruce and that spider and Francis Drake and the King of Spain's beard. I'd mention 1066 because it's memorable, and 1666 because it's easy and also the Fire of London. Having acted all the wives of Henry VIII, I'm fairly *au courant*

with the Tudors and can chatter glibly about the
Stuarts, having acted six of the lady friends of
Charles II . . . a very curtailed acquaintance with
that monarch, I admit. This would lead to
Queen Anne who was responsible for a lot of
furniture, also a lot of children . . . thirteen to
be exact, though who exactly *King* Anne was, I
haven't the foggiest notion, unless he was one of
those Electors of Hanover who in my pretty scat-
terbrain are all mixed up with something called
the Hanseatic League and the Council of Trent.
Or do I mean the Treaty of Ghent? Maybe I'm
thinking of the Diet of Worms . . . although I'd
rather not. It would be pleasant to gossip a bit
about George IV and Mrs. Fitzherbert as well
as talk a little scandal about Nelson and Lady
Hamilton because this would give me the chance
to paint some charming vignettes of Brighton
and Bath, the beaux Brummel and Nash, David
Garrick and Sarah Siddons and further crucial
moments in Britain's chronicle. What else? Oh
yes, the South Sea Bubble, the Irish Potato Fam-
ine, the Black Hole of Calcutta and the War of
Jenkins' Ear — only I didn't know who Jenkins
was — and what was the matter with his ear?

France's history, I imagine, would come out
on a par with England's. There would be special

emphasis on the three last Louis' and their expensive lady friends, a lot of good healthy gore
concerning the Revolution and a learned study
of Louis Napoleon and the Second Empire owing
to the fact that I once acted the role of the Em-
press Eugénie. How broadening the theatre is,
to be sure! Never having done any Italian shows,
I'd have to limit the Renaissance to the Medicis
and the Borgias. As for Spain . . . well, Ferdi-
nand, Isabella and the Columbus bit and to hell
with the rest.

So much for Europe, I thought. But then
something in my wakeful brain said "What about
Russia?" Russia? Yes, Russia. *Tiens, tiens!*
Well, there was Peter the Great who was Great,
and Ivan the Terrible who was Terrible, and
Catherine the Great who was also Great, but in a
more intimate fashion, and Boris Godunov who
was an opera, and Christina of Sweden who was
Greta Garbo. This brought me bang up against
the Scandinavian countries, which I'd forgotten
all about, not that I've ever learned very much
to forget. Norway? Leif Erikson. Denmark?
Hans Andersen, also Hamlet. Finland? Sibelius.
Iceland? Don't be funny! Better skip Scandina-
via for the moment. Take a few other countries.
Poland, for instance. Poland . . . Mme. Walew-

ska, Chopin and countless patriots many of whom have never seen Poland. Holland? Rembrandt, Hendrick Hudson, Hans Brinker and that little boy who held his finger in the dyke.

This profitless reviewing was wearing me out and now a soothing streak of dawn stole into the room like a cool draught of Miltown. I realized that I had still to take up the Near East and tried sleepily to go over a stanza or two from the Rubáiyát. Also, I had done nothing about the Far East. But who was I to do anything about the Far East? Anyway, I figured as I drifted off to sleep, by the time my class got to that point in history we'd have finished our stay on the desert island. Someone would have come to our rescue . . . undoubtedly the United States Marines. And the United States Marines wouldn't have any use for history. They're supposed to make it.

. . . attached to the wrong body . . .

I Never Remember
a Name
But
I Always Forget
a Face

I am continually amazed at the emphasis there is in this country on the desperate importance of always knowing a person's name. Not merely knowing it, but showing off the fact by repeating it over and over in a manner both eagerly precocious and completely unnecessary. The repetitive insistence with which our bright business boys intersperse their end of any conversation with "Yes, R.B.," "What was that, R.B.?" "You're a card, R.B." is curiously reminiscent of the old vaudeville "That was Elmer" telephone routine. If I sound somewhat sour on this subject, it's because I am. And if I fail to share the national zest for the reiterated use of a person's name it's because I am totally unable to do so, being totally unable to remember names. I am further soured by that old cliché about never remembering a name but never forgetting a face (which is on a bromidic par with "I know nothing about Art, but I know what I like"). Because all too frequently I don't even remember a face. Or I remember it attached to the wrong body. Or identified with the wrong locale.

If my memory as a whole were shaky, I'd be seriously concerned . . . well, maybe not too seriously so, for then I'd be in the state of grace of the happy half-wit. I recall with detailed minutiae events, even unimportant ones, in my life or in the lives of my friends. I can sing every word of popular songs of a vintage riper than I'd like to admit. I can drive without making one wrong turning along a complicated motor route I've been over only once, or describe each course of a meal I had in Paris ten years ago. I can tell you in order the correct names of the dead Kings of England. I just can't tell you the correct names of living commoners. Or the faces that go with them.

It isn't that people don't make an impression on me. They do and sometimes it's a whale of an impression. Once I've identified an individual, even someone I hardly know, I can carry on splendidly with a stream of social insincerities which would rate me a *summa cum laude* at any Success School, giving forth with how lovely it is to see them AGAIN, and how I did enjoy that lobster Newburg and how is that charming Mrs. Snooks. However, let charming Mrs. Snooks turn up some time later and in a locale other than the one in which she rightfully belongs and I wouldn't know her from Mrs. Doakes.

For an itinerant member of the theatrical profession, people are always "turning up." Friends, relatives and chance acquaintances. If they didn't, it would be sad indeed. Relatives and friends, of course, are to be happily expected . . . most of them, that is. It's those chance acquaintances who add to the burden of an actor's life. Particularly the ones who don't take into account the passage of years. Persons whose hair was once raven can't suddenly arrive with pure white hair — or, what's even worse, with no hair at all — and say "You know, you haven't changed at all" . . .

without risking the rejoinder of "Well, Toots, you sure have!"

Such was the situation last winter in a midwestern city when there burst into my dressing room a handsome, smartly dressed woman with the glad cry of *"Darling!* I'll bet you never expected to see me here!" Her betting was so right. I never expected to see her there . . . or anywhere, for I hadn't the remotest idea who she was. She did look vaguely familiar and I managed to force out a "For heaven's sake, he*llo!*" and to assume an expression of delighted astonishment. With outstretched hands she grasped both of mine and held on to them so long we looked as though we were about to go into the opening steps of a folk dance. Beaming with the glee of someone who has just pulled off a successful surprise . . . as indeed she had . . . she burbled "Can you *believe* it? After all these years?" I said no I couldn't and, hoping for an enlightening clue, added "Just how many years is it?"

"Oh!" she cried in mock dismay. "Don't let's say!" We didn't. "All you have to do is look at this!" and she patted her chic hairdo. The color was gray with a dash of bluing. I wigged her mentally . . . blond, brown, red, with no resulting glimmer. Moreover she was further disguised by a deep suntan. As she explained, "We're just back from Florida."

"And how was Florida?" I inquired politely.

"Oh darling!" she shrugged. "You know Florida."

I knew Florida all right, but I still didn't know her. We floundered along, inanely on my part. She told me that I looked wonderful and I told her that she did too, on the likelihood that she probably did. She said that they hardly ever got to New York any more and I said that that was too bad. She recalled what great old fun we'd had that time and I restrained the impulse to ask *what* time and *what* great old fun and who the hell is *we?* Mercifully she had a commuter's train to catch, for suddenly she glanced at her watch, leapt to her feet, gave me a goodbye hug and said "George sends his love."

"Dear George!" I responded warmly. "Do give him mine!"

My stage manager who overheard our parting words asked me who my good friend was. I had to admit that his guess was as good as mine. Since which time he and I have adopted the phrase "George sends his love" as a code signal for "Don't ask me who the hell this creature is!"

Curiously enough, persons I knew during girl-hood days are usually no problem. The alacrity with which I recall them astonishes me myself. There may be times, to be sure, when I feel the way Ethel Barrymore apparently did when upon the announcement that a former schoolmate was waiting to see her, sighed "All right! Wheel her in!" It's the people I have met during recent years who present the worst problems, especially those who refuse to stay in their associated setting and expect to be recognized. No wonder the con-vention boys and girls wear those coffin-plate-like labels on their lapels subtly proclaiming their identity. If only a person would come forth with some helpful reminder like "Last time was in Tacoma, *remember?*" then maybe I would. Or "Have you heard from the So-and-So's lately?" And I'd get along swimmingly with some tactful hint such as "Haven't seen you since we both got slightly squiffed in Springfield." What's more, in the instance of a name like Springfield, that Smith of American towns, they ought also to spec-ify the state.

I once spent several delightful hours in the home of a charming lady from Princeton, Illinois, and she is really the motivation for my writing this piece. In fact, I'd like to request any chance

reader who hails from Princeton Illinois to bring
it to the attention of each and every hostess of
that town in the hopes that the right one will
see it and perhaps absolve me of the guilt feeling of years. What her name is I couldn't
possibly tell you, after all this time. I couldn't possibly have told you one month after my pleasant
stay with her in Princeton, *Illinois,* because, as I
have already indicated, in regard to names my
mind is a sieve with a large hole in it. When one
evening in New York she put in an appearance
backstage, it was clear to me that her face had
followed her name right on out through the hole.
I am afraid that it was all too clear to her also,
for after I had floundered vaguely about as I had
in the case of my George-sends-his-love friend,
the kindly lady came to my aid by gently suggest-
ing "Princeton. Remember?" I said "Why of
course!" in what I fear was a hollow tone, and
dutifully concentrated my thoughts on the
Athens of New Jersey . . . the ivy-wreathed build-
ings of Old Nassau, the people there whom I
knew . . . even those I never knew, Dr. Einstein
and Woodrow Wilson. Not a glimmer. The
visit was awkwardly strained and the poor lady
left somewhat abruptly. One minute after her
departure the light dawned and with a loud cry

of "Princeton ILLINOIS!" I rushed out after her to
the stage door. But by then she was engulfed in
the Broadway shuffle and I was clad in only a
dressing gown and slippers. Why hadn't she *said*
Princeton Illinois? And what is Illinois doing
with a Princeton anyway? Probably named by
some hysterically loyal graduate who never
emerged from the chrysalis of the coonskin coat.

Encountering a foreigner away from his own
country can be pretty baffling too. Several years
ago on an Italian train I ran into a distinguished-
looking Frenchman who obviously knew me, for
as I entered the compartment (first class) he
jumped to his feet and bowed. I had the feeling
that I knew him too so I bowed back. We
shook hands, uttered the French equivalent of
"Fancy meeting you here!" and thereupon entered into a sprightly conversation. He was, it
seemed, *en vacance* and on his way to visit a
cousin near Como. We talked of the beauties
of northern Italy, of the international situation,
of the bicycle *tour de France* and of the legs
of Josephine Baker. That is, he talked. I was
too distracted trying to think who he was to con-
tribute more than monosyllabic responses. At
lunch we found ourselves sharing the same table
and I found myself accepting his offer of a li-
queur. His attitude was one of punctilious de-

corum, which was just as it should have been, although I rather regretted the fact, as the gentleman was quite handsome. I kept cudgeling my brains. Where had I met this elegant Monsieur? At some function in Washington? Crossing on the *Ile de France*? I even toyed with the possibility of the Fourth of July tea party at the American Embassy, although he seemed much too grand for that. Being the female counterpart of Casper Milquetoast, I seldom if ever have the nerve to come out candidly and say "Look, friend, let's have it. Who are you?" But this situation was too tormenting. As the train pulled into Turin, I admitted with what I hoped was pretty confusion that I was *désolée* to be such an *imbécile*, I knew him well of course, but would he enlighten me as to where we'd last met? He said certainly and mentioned the modest Left Bank hotel which I usually patronize. "I am the concièrge there," he added, "and many times I have handed Madame her letters and messages." Madame thought with a shock of how many times she had handed him back a tip and wondered how she would ever face him when he was once more back in his green coat and brass buttons. Madame solved the situation by stopping next time at another hotel.

As a matter of fact, many persons in mufti,

as it were, are somewhat of a shock. The hospital nurse whom one has seen only in starched uniform and cap suddenly emerging from a swimming pool with wet hair and bare midriff produces the impression of a renegade nun who has just jumped over the wall. And one night at the opera I nearly dropped in my tracks when I learned that the glorious creature in white tie and tails was the surgeon whom last I had beheld in white skullcap, dangling gauze mask and butcher blouse, bending over my bed of pain to admire the fine needlework he had done on my abdomen. Truth to tell, he didn't know me either. It's not surprising that doctors face a like dilemma. My women friends often complain woefully that our mutual obstetrician never recognizes them at cocktail parties. Well, after all, an obstetrician is one person who might perhaps be forgiven for not remembering a face.

In my own case . . . and the more I survey my own case the more serious it appears . . . the change of season has an unfortunate effect upon the memory. It seems downright indecent to imagine in the overcoat and muffler-swathed figure one encounters on Fifth Avenue in a blizzard the bronzed, semi-naked god one so admired last summer on Malibu Beach. Running into former holiday acquaintances under cold-weather conditions, I've caught myself about to say "Good Lord! I didn't know you with your clothes on!"

That literally was true for a friend of mine when, shortly after she had moved to Philadelphia to live, an endearing and socially prominent hostess invited her to spend an afternoon and evening out at their country estate. The occasion was an annual outing of the hostess's intimate circle and it would be a means of introducing my friend to some "nice Philadelphians." My friend, who had a job in the city, arrived at the country estate in midafternoon and was informed by a butler that the ladies were all down at the swimming pool. Indeed they were. Ten superb Philadelphia dowagers, clad in nothing other than bathing caps. Formal introductions were in order, the proud names of the Quaker City's first families rolled forth as each dripping arm was extended and in no time at all my friend in an equal state of undress was splashing merrily in their pagan midst carefully addressing each elderly Nereid by her proper surname. At five o'clock a whistle from the hostess's husband announced the fact that the gentlemen were ready to disport themselves, and swathed in bath-towel togas the ladies retired to the house to rest and fix up for dinner. At cocktail time they reassembled, beautifully gowned, exquisitely groomed, and my friend was completely unable to identify a single one of them.

Sometimes I do remember a face and it proves to be that of someone I've never met in my life. There was that time I sat down at a dining-car table opposite a white-bearded gentleman whose magnificent features were strikingly familiar and I was saved from exclaiming "Well for the love of Mike, look who's here!" only by the timely arrival of the steward who bowed deferentially and asked, "What will it be today, Mr. Chief Justice?" You're right. It was Charles Evans Hughes.

And there was also the time when that enchanting and profoundly lamented actor Roland Young, also on a train, was disturbed while reading an engrossing book by a persistent fellow passenger who kept crossing the aisle to hover above his chair insisting that they must have met somewhere. The face was so familiar. Was it at the furniture convention in Chicago? Or that West Indian cruise two years ago? Or wasn't he on the dais at the big Rotary banquet last month? Roland, always loathe to reveal his professional identity, answered each query in his "cocained upper lip" fashion with a clipped "No. I think not." In a final desperate effort the man announced, "Well, I'm G. B. Blank of the Blank Company of Hartford Connecticut." Roland looked up solemnly, replied "So am I," and went on reading his book.

My faulty memory worries me, although I'm really not losing any sleep over it. What I am losing, I suppose, is friends and I also suppose I should do something about it. There are those memory courses one hears about where one learns how to retain a name through all sorts of complicated and rather idiotic associations. But life is short and there are so many pleasanter courses I'd like to find the time to take, like Spanish and cooking and Oriental Art and I've always wanted to learn tap dancing. Moreover, for all the experts who guarantee that they can teach you how to remember a name, how many can claim to be able to teach you how to remember a face? Come to think of it, there are quite a few faces I'd prefer not to learn how to remember. So maybe, in spite of everything I'm just as well off.

...she has to inspect all those guardsmen...

Production-Line Courtesy

Once upon a plane trip, I sat directly back of a little old lady who was giving every indication that this was her first experience in air travel and that as far as she was concerned, it might well prove to be her last. The flight happened to be an uneventfully calm one . . . so much so that the captain felt free to take time out in the main cabin for that routine stroll down the aisle to carry on that routine chitchat with each passenger. When came the old lady's turn, he leaned over her chair and with a pleasant smile enquired politely, "Is everything all right?" The poor little soul jumped as though she'd been jabbed with an ice pick. "Is everything all RIGHT?" she squealed in a note of near hysteria. "You're asking *me?* YOU ought to know!"

I could sympathize with her sentiments completely. Hers was the reply I have wanted time and again to make, but have always lacked the nerve. Mind you, I am all in favor of the pilot's personal visit. It makes for an agreeable distraction . . . especially if he happens to be a comely pilot . . . and besides, it's always reassuring to feel that so long as he's being sociable there's nothing too seriously wrong with the engines. What bothers me is that is-everything-all-right opener. Although, come to think of it, if I were a pilot (a dim likelihood) I daresay I should find myself hard put to know how to start a brief causerie with each of these total strangers. "Have you read any good books lately?" or "What is your opinion of our foreign policy?" might lead to too much involvement for the allotted time. It would not be surprising to learn that Queen Elizabeth faces the same problem when she has to inspect all those guardsmen and say a word of cheer to each. I'm willing to bet, however, that she doesn't ask each man if everything is all right. It's not that I'm complaining about the pilot's conversational limitations. After all, one expects him to be less a master of repartee than an expert in aviation. His moment of attention is flattering, but what takes the edge off is his feeling obliged to lavish the same attention, conveyed by the same formula, on every other passenger.

Courtesy is fine and heaven knows we need more and more of it in a rude and frenetic world, but mechanized courtesy is as pallid as Pablum . . . in fact, it isn't even courtesy. One can put up with "Service with a Smile" if the smile is genuine and not mere compulsory tooth-baring. And while I am hardly advocating "Service with a Snarl," I find myself occasionally wishing for "Service with a Deadpan," or just plain Service, executed with efficiency and minus all the Charm School garnish.

Take the world of travel. In my profession I happen to have to take it a lot. I also happen to be one of those fast-disappearing eccentrics, a railroad enthusiast. As such it grieves me to find this type of IBM politeness policy taking over our dining cars . . . not in regard to the waiters, but as far as the chief steward is concerned. One gets the impression that all chief stewards have been ordered to conform to a booklet of rules, a major one being:

At least once, and preferably twice during every meal, approach each individual patron (a good moment is when said patron's mouth is full of food) and inquire pleasantly but firmly how he or she is getting along.

During recent years I have consumed countless meals in countless dining cars and have yet to get through one without the head steward barging in on not only my food but my reading matter to ask either with hollow concern or with embarrassing cheer how I am getting along. It makes me feel I'm just learning how to handle a fork. By way of occasional variation he may say "Is the fish O.K.?" . . . and if it weren't wouldn't he have heard of it, just! Or else the most disquieting "Are you all right?" as though I were exhibiting symptoms of some oncoming seizure.

Not long ago during a first breakfast aboard a California-bound streamliner, when the chief steward with fearful heartiness asked "How are the eggs?" I did muster up the courage to answer "Scrambled" . . . not, I'm afraid, without a certain fine splutter, my mouth, of course, being at the time replete. This had a silencing effect on him for the remainder of the meal and he even allowed me to eat my lunch without trying to find out how I was getting along. At dinner, however, he was back with the same old pitch and when he ambushed me with an aggressively glad "Enjoying your steak?" I meekly complied with a "Very much, thank you," because, as a matter of fact, I was.

The trouble with these regimented individual touches is that there's nothing individual about them. It's not as if the steward were implying that he has singled me out as a person of such rare charm and distinction he couldn't resist lavishing special solicitude upon me. He lavishes the same solicitude, expressed in the same patter, upon the fat lady across the aisle softly shedding crumbs on her bosom, the pale female wanly nibbling celery at the next table and the salesman who is getting polluted down at the end of the car. It makes you realize that as long as he is executing his courtesy-by-rote, he doesn't give a hoot in hell whether you're really enjoying your meal or whether it's giving you acute ptomaine.

As a railroad addict, there is a further "service" which I, for one, deplore . . . namely the intercom public address system which has invaded the erstwhile quiet of our extra-fare super-trains. It may be helpful for pointing out Nature's Wonderland along the way and it's nice to learn that at Albuquerque you'll have ten minutes and a chance to purchase that pair of genuine Indian moccasins. But then some bright boy had to get overly smart and think up the added "service" of canned music which you can turn off in your own bedroom but not in the adjacent ones, nor in the lounge car, the diner or Vista-Dome. This last innovation is for all travelers a genuine delight and it would seem the ideal setting for scenic enjoyment without a distracting background of "Music-to-Look-By." I don't believe that the Rockies appear any more imposing against a mood accompaniment of "Tea for Two," and the strains of "The Last Time I Saw Paris" isn't going to make the Panhandle of Texas look like anything but the Panhandle of Texas. True, once en route to San Diego, as we streaked past the famous old mission of San Juan, our ears were caressed by the vocal of "When the Swallows Come Back to Capistrano," but such miracles don't happen often.

Then there are stations. For over a century and a half since the launching of the first locomotive steam engine, travelers in railway stations have managed in some way or another to locate outgoing and incoming trains without benefit of the loudspeaker. Now comes this earsplitting blessing to itinerant mankind and I guess it's a great idea . . . that is if one can make out what the hell is being announced. Most station announcers have a distressing way of placing their mouths directly upon the microphone and yelling. What is further distressful is the recent innovation of some canned "Courtesy" to add to the general cacophony. Last winter in an upstate depot I sat listening with throbbing eardrums to the train schedule announcements. To my fascination, at the finish of each bulletin, there blared forth a coy little tag line to the effect that the New York Central System wished us each and every one a happy journey and expressed the sincere hope that we would enjoy our trip on the New York Central System. I had a sudden vision of a board meeting of the directors of this time-honored and distinguished line listening to detailed reports concerning the varying moods of its clientele, evincing serious concern over the words of a conductor as he relayed the disturbing information that a woman rode all the way from Harmon to Albany staring at the beauties of the Hudson and never cracking a single smile of contentment, while a porter spread panic in the meeting with the news that one male passenger had got off at Poughkeepsie scowling and muttering things.

That each member of the board of the big public utilities is concerned over the personal felicity of each patron is as pretty a sentiment as the notion that Conrad Hilton is wrapped up emotionally in the spiritual welfare of each client . . . pardon me, *guest* . . . in his hotels.

At least in hotels, this form of regimented courtesy is confined largely to those innumerable items of instructive literature printed on bits of cardboard and scattered in profusion about every room . . . on the bureau, on the writing desk, above the nightstand and under the glass top of every table. Start reading them all and you're gone for the afternoon. They might not be so bad if they weren't, most of them, couched in such fancy language. There is always one, to be sure, which isn't, and that is the bluntly inexorable notification that CHECK-OUT TIME IS 3 P.M. The rest are arch as anything to be found in a Cape Cod Gift Shoppe. The simple fact that you may order tomorrow's breakfast "TO-NITE" is illustrated by that symbol of urban awakening, the crowing

cock, plus a lot of guff about being called by your
cheery morning waiter (it's always "your" . . . why
do they want to give us these people?) bringing
you that "fresh-squeezed, ice-cold fruit juice,"
those "farm-fresh fried eggs," that "sizzling, crispy
bacon," that "crunchy, munchy toast" and "oh
Boy, that roast-oven, tangy, piping hot coffee."
Any cheery morning waiter who would mention
such goodies to me would receive the tangy, roast-
oven coffee full in the face. The local ordinance
not to smoke in bed is, in certain hotels, made to
appear less harsh by the pretty illustration of a
gentleman stepping out through a doorway with
a smart but rather tubular lady who, on closer
inspection, proves to be a cigarette in feminine
attire, and under this the gentle injunction,
"Please don't let her go out alone." They don't
take up the question of cigars or pipes. Then
there are all the overelaborated bits of information about dining, transportation and television
facilities, the fact that "Clean Clothes Pack
Easier" which, while it may defy elegant gram-
mar, at least identifies the laundry bag, and dangling from a cabinet hook in the bathroom a small
envelope for used razor blades gimmicked up with
the portrait of a maid in lacy cap and apron, like
something out of a 1910 farce, staring with dismay

at her semi-amputated finger. In the desk drawer amid the plethora of stationery, telegraph blanks, Don't Disturb signs, stickers and an unfinished letter left by the last occupant starting out "Dear Hazel," one occasionally finds a sheet of paper at the top of which is printed "Your complete comfort and satisfaction is our most earnest desire" and further tender avowals which eventually lead to the realization that this is a complaint-and-suggestion slip to be turned in to some mythical creature of goodwill whose every waking moment is dedicated to your health, comfort and happiness while under this roof. That Messers Hilton, Sheraton, Statler, Kirkaby, Knott and the rest of the Mine Host chain gang want their patrons to be satisfied is understandable, since what they really want is their continued patronage. But why must their public relations henchmen express this desire in printed missives which are just short of being love letters?

The coy printed word is not confined to paper or cardboard. Last week I spent some time soaking in a hot tub speculating about the interesting reading matter which appeared in raised rubber letters on a mat hanging beside the shower. "This shower mat," it said, "was placed here for your protection, to make your stay with us more enjoyable." How, I ask you, can one go about enjoying a shower mat? And what do they mean by *protection?* Protection from slipping and cracking open your skull and thereby making your stay more enjoyable? Why not the simple words "Shower mat" for the benefit of some benighted yokel who perhaps may never have seen such civilized amenities, and have done with it . . . or, if you like, stand on it?

Factory-made courtesy has even invaded the realm of the highway road signs. As if the advertisement billboards, Burma-Shave jingles and Heated Cabins signs were not litter enough, we have those eyecatchers on the outskirts of small towns saying "Thank you. Come again." Thank you for what? Driving through the town as rapidly as the law permits? Come again, for what? To repeat the same hurried process?

And how about those self-congratulatory little placards such as one sees in certain taxicabs, heralding the man behind the wheel to be "Your courteous driver"? Why not let the passenger discover this admirable quality? For that matter, why not have the passenger wear a large convention button reading "Your courteous passenger"? To me, even more nauseous is the commercialized word "Friendly." Any shop which would advertise itself as being "Your Friendly Butcher" I would make it a point to boycott. Why should a butcher stress the Dale Carnegie merits of his character rather than the merits of his merchandise? As a matter of fact, my own butcher happens to be an extremely friendly one, or rather, and better still, we are good friends owing to natural selection and years of pleasant acquaintance between counter and raised cleaver. He is a proud and masterly tradesman who requires no promotional gimmick. His shingle bears simply his name and the words "Quality Meats" and he would no more announce himself as being anyone's "Friendly Butcher" than my attorney would have "Your Friendly Lawyer" printed on his professional card.

Or maybe I'm wrong. Maybe this is the direction in which we are headed. Maybe along with packaged frozen foods we'll be able, when we feel the need, to go to some deep-freeze and extract a chunk of frozen friendship. Ah me! I'd better start refurbishing my professional brochures and publicity material and have the printers insert after my name "Your Friendly Actress." When that day arrives, I trust someone will send for "My Friendly Mortician."

. . . the smiles of forced cheer . . .

If You're Going to Go, Go!

How often has one watched some well-intentioned but misguided soul waiting about on a station platform to see off a friend who is already aboard the train . . . a train, moreover, which seems destined never to depart? It appears as one of the most awkward and meaningless gestures of human behavior. The spasmodic nods of the head and wavings of the hand, the smiles of forced cheer, the occasional coyly blown kiss, the gyrations of pantomime and facial contortions in futile attempts to communicate through the thick glass of a Pullman window and the unexpressed but obvious mutual wish to heaven that the train would start bear ludicrous witness to the idiocy of the convention of seeing people off on trains. Or, for that matter, on any other vehicle of transportation.

The impulse to see friends off on a ship is more understandable. There is an element of romantic adventure in going down to the docks. It is pleasant to enjoy a brief inspection of an ocean liner and pleasant too if the departing friends insist on sharing a farewell cup of cheer in their cabin even if the cup has perforce to be the toothbrush glass. But after the final "All Visitors Ashore" warning has sounded, all visitors should go not only ashore, but away. Few people, however, have that much sense. They feel it their duty to stand with aching feet on the pier while their friends on board ship feel compelled to return the courtesy by leaning with wilting bodies over the rail to exchange grotesque gestures and shouted inanities for what seems like hours and hours and hours. Once you have said goodbye to your friends and have gone ashore, keep on going. That is if you want them to remain your friends. If, of course, you're the sort of person who can't resist watching a great vessel back out, with foghorn blasting into the North River (and I admit it's quite a sight to resist) keep hidden until the mighty craft is well under way, then step out from behind your pillar. By this time, you'll be a mere dot amid the melee of foolish wellwishers jamming the pier, and, in all probability, your dear friends will have fled from the deck in search of restorative below.

Seeing off friends at an airport is almost as bad; even if once they are safely through the gate, there is happily little chance for communication either vocal or pantomimic. There is, however, prior to this moment of release, the excruciating tedium of all that waiting around which plane travel entails. Most persons arrive at airports well ahead of time and most airports, with their frenetic crowds, their scarcity of seats or benches, their absolute dearth of quiet places in which to escape the loud cacophony of the incessant loudspeaker, are hardly ideal settings for tender farewells. Sensible people should get these over with either at home or in the bus terminal.

It is not only at times of travel departure that

human beings have not the intelligence and sensitivity *to* depart, there are many who seem incapable of departing from a party, an informal gathering or even a casual call. These are the ones who at a reasonably conventional hour after dinner will glance at their watches, leap to their feet with the guilty apprehension of the soldier who realizes he has a scant twenty minutes in which to return to barracks before taps, say heavens above they *must* be going along, and where is it they go? It's usually into the outer hallway where, after bustling into wraps and coats, they come to a dead halt. And there they linger because they all at once recall an anecdote they've forgotten to tell you, or they feel obliged to repeat some of the ones they've already told you, and there you stand on one foot, then the other, trying to make polite response and hoping that the wan leer on your face is concealing the ardent wish in your heart that they'd get the hell on out. Often as not the departing guests perform their delayed action either on the threshold or just outside of your open front door. This means that if you live in a city apartment, the elevator man who has been rung for, and is already waiting on the landing, is forced to become an unwilling mem-

ber of the merry group. And if, in fact, the
group is too merry and the hour too nocturnal,
next morning the building superintendent sends
a cautionary notice that the adjacent tenants have
complained. If you are an exurbanite, the delayed departer and the open front door offer
more rural inconveniences. In winter, icy blasts
whoosh through your house as you stand for
shivering minutes (the slow departers are, of
course, completely bundled in their coats) feeling the skeletal clutch of pneumonia at your
chest and listening less to what is being said than
to the click of the thermostat and the buzz of
the oil burner valiantly consuming extra fuel.
In summer, the screen door yawns wide in open-
house welcome to the myriad specimens of in-
sect life which have been swarming all evening
about the porch light.

Sometimes these dawdling departers, after they
have finally gone, don't know how to stay gone.
The re-entry of a husband who has been sent back
to reclaim his wife's forgotten purse, or of a lady
friend making an apologetic reappearance because oh dear she finds she is minus one glove
is not only an anticlimax to a pleasant evening,
it can can be a definite shock. This is especially
so when the host and hostess are rehashing the

party with highly personal comments about each guest and may even have removed a few of their outer garments preparatory to retiring for the night.

It grieves me to admit that the most pernicious of non-goers are usually members of my own sex. Take, for example, the woman who attends a concert or a play and who, during intermission, goes out for a smoke or a stroll in the lobby. The trouble is that she seldom gets to the lobby. She will arrive halfway across an exit and here she encounters an acquaintance who in turn is another non-goer, and there the two of them form a barricade against all egress at the start of the intermission or ingress when the bell warns that the curtain is about to go up. Then there is that Menace of the Department Store, the female shopper. She too is a threshold loiterer and where she loiters is halfway out and halfway in the elevator while deliberately she peers about to see whether or not she is getting off at the right floor. And of course there should be a plain-clothes guardian of the law at the top of every escalator to pounce upon those homicidal maniacs who step off that always somewhat frightening contraption and who, having made that one step, take no further ones until they have slowly gotten their bearings or consulted their shopping lists or plunged into their handbags for their compacts.

Oh well, we can't all be perfect, I suppose. Only the other night when starting off for dinner at the house of some neighbors, my husband astonished and somewhat wounded me too when he announced in the tone of an invading commander stating his terms, "Now when we start to go, I don't care how long you dawdle gabbing with Nancy, *I* for one, am going to GO!"

...the same sort of prestige as owning a Picasso...

The
Limitations
of Word
Dropping

I wonder how many intellectually indolent persons there are beside myself who go blithely through life hearing, reading, even using words or phrases without really knowing what they mean. Styles in language come in with their attendant snobberies like styles in painting or styles in show dogs and there are a lot of fancy words going the rounds these days. To be a successful word dropper lends one the same sort of prestige as owning a Picasso or a Weimaraner. The egghead in me (which consists in no vestige of yolk and only a dab of the white) has incited me to master a few of these stylish terms, although I'm far from being in the Picasso-Weimaraner owner category. I can toss off *catalyst*, also *polemics* and *empathy*, and pretty pleased I've been about them too. That is, until an insensitive member of my family, fed up with hearing me air the latter, quelled my enthusiasm by singing "You need empathy . . . empathy, just empathy," which has rendered me a little shy about an overuse of modish words. I would, however, dearly love to be able to bandy *euphoric* about only I wouldn't know when or in what connection to bandy it. *Ic* surely is a suffix implying *in regard* or *relating to* something. Well then, does *euphoric* mean in regard or relating to *euphors?* And what *are* euphors? I really do know that *euphoric* has to do with *euphoria* which is, I believe, some sort of state of being although it sounds more like a town in the state of Kansas.

Another *ic* word one hears every now and then is *kinetic*. Now what is *kinetic* in regard or relating to? The early motion picture industry in Germany when a movie house was known as a *kino* palace? And a further puzzler is *dialectic,* which apparently hasn't anything to do with spoken dialects, but is far more eclectic (you see? I can get off a few of these highbrow *ics* myself even if it has taken me some little time to get around to eclectic!). But to continue with *dialectic* . . . whoever uses that I consider a definite show-off. As for anyone who would say *dialectically ambivalent,* well that's the sort of creature who would corner one at a cocktail party and talk about Thorstein Veblen and I seldom attract that sort of creature into a corner. By way of confession, I have just looked up *dialectically ambivalent* in the dictionary and I still don't know what it means; and judging by the printed interpretation, it wouldn't surprise me to learn that the writers of the dictionary didn't exactly know either.

Another stylish adjective which eludes my grasp is *empirical.* I guess that I must look up *empirical* at least a couple of times a year but the definition never sticks. It can't be very interesting. *Specious* is another baffler, albeit it's no real problem, for while it might be gratifying to write *specious,* it's doubtful if I'd ever utter it. People could think I was saying *spacious* with a Bronx accent.

There are a few chic adjectives, to be sure, whose meanings I do know but which I am inclined to invest with further meaning. Take for example *uxorial* and *uxorious*. I know that *uxorial* means "wifely" and that *uxorious* means "devoted to a wife." But what a wife! Downright depraved the way they go uxing after each other all over the house!

Another word I endow with peculiar significance is *caucus*. I know all right that a caucus is a meeting. But I can't dismiss the idea that it's a meeting of crows. It could also be a meeting of starlings. In fact I never watch or hear one of those chattering, fluttering, jibbering wing-happy flocks squabbling for overnight roosts on some city building (and I'll say this for starlings . . . they'll always pick a building of distinction like the Public Library or the Metropolitan Museum of Art) without thinking, Oh look! A caucus of starlings!

A substantive used now and then by the literary wise guys is *nexus*. I have just looked up *nexus* and find that it means a connection between individuals of a group. It sounds more like the result of an even closer connection between a Texan and a water nixie. And every so often some show-off will word-drop *xenopho-*

bia, which I presume means fear of or hatred for *xenos.* But then I'm not especially interested in xenos.

There is the frightfully impressive term *categorical imperative.* And that I'm not going to look up, partly because if I were to find out what it means and use it, my dear ones would never let me get away with it, partly because I'd be sure to be disillusioned. For in my mind's eye, I cherish the picture of a Roman tyrant in imperial purple and golden laurel wreath thundering forth a *categorical imperative* from the summit of the Capitoline Hill.

This tasty picture of Rome brings thoughts of the Latin words and phrases which crop up hither and yon in the conversation of the smart literati and whose correct usage it would be gratifying to know. Certain ones of course are easy and it's not difficult to rattle off *ipso facto, de mortuis, in vino veritas* and *e pluribus unum* although there are not too many conversations during which *e pluribus unum* comes in handy. But while I may be confident about *ipso facto,* I'm pretty insecure about *de facto* and my dictionary only adds to the insecurity by saying "actual: as *de facto* government: distinguished from *de jure"* because I'm not exactly up on *de jure.* I had four years of Latin in school and college and I can still stagger through a rough translation of most phrases in common usage but where does it get one to have figured out that *a priori* means "from prior" or that *sine qua non* means "without which not"? As for *deus ex machina,* that obviously refers to a "god out of a machine." Well, who was the god and what sort of a machine was it and what was he doing in it in the first place? As for *quid pro quo* I wouldn't have the foggiest notion what that's about unless it's some classical allusion to chewing tobacco.

Not perhaps so stylishly up to date, but equally impressive is some ecclesiastical terminology which occasionally leaps from churchly circles over into lay ones. Spiritual and temporal is not hard to grasp but my own grasp goes limp when it makes a stab at *Canon Law.* I know that it has nothing to do with ordinance. To me Canon Law is a learned and Right Reverend divine connected with the Church of Scotland. As for Papal Bull, that obviously must belong in the domestic animal department of the Vatican and it would not surprise me to hear of a Papal Cow grazing in a quiet cloister back of St. Peter's.

Doubtless originating in churchly confines and

now let loose in literate circles is something
or someone known as the Devil's Advocate. How
very medieval! But when and under what circumstances does one call upon a Devil's Advocate?
And what is a Printer's Devil? What, for that
matter, is housemaid's knee?

The more I delve into the depressing subject of my limited linguistics, the more I become
aware that in addition to these high-toned words
there are any number of sayings and adages which
I have heard and read from childhood, which
I may even have used, without knowing exactly
what they mean. Take for instance that one
about "he who runs may read," or to quote
it accurately . . . for it seems first to have been
pronounced by someone named Habakkuk . . .
"that he may run who readeth it," which still
doesn't make it any clearer. Why did whoever
he was have to run? Was whatever he read so
horrifying he felt obliged to rush away? Or was
it an item of reading matter so absorbing he
took it along on his run? Like those zany ads
showing people in racing shorts sprinting and
leaping hurdles while holding at arm's length
newspapers spread wide before them to show
that "in Philadelphia nearly everybody reads the
Bulletin." Another time-honored apothegm (and

don't think I'm not proud of knowing that one even if I don't quite know how to pronounce it!) is the thing about somebody being "hoist with his own petard," which to me is incomprehensible. Isn't it also slightly ungrammatical? Shouldn't it be "hoisted"? or am I thinking of "foist"? Or am I even thinking? And where is he hoist (or hoisted or foist) to? And does "with his own petard" mean that the petard goes along with him? Or does the petard do the hoisting (or foisting)? And what is a petard anyway? Again my deranged mind's eye pictures a pirate ship and some unfortunate wretch dangling from the yardarm while the Jolly Roger flutters in the breeze. Maybe I'm confusing the Jolly Roger with whatever a petard is. Come to think of it, what is a *canard?* aside from being a French duck? Maybe I'm mixing my metaphors. Maybe someone is "hoist with his own canard." Oh the hell with it!

Then there's that expression about getting something "straight from the horse's mouth." Now horses are certainly among the earth's most beautiful creatures, but have you ever taken a good look inside one of their mouths? Especially one that has yellow teeth and a lot of greenish gunk slathered about in it? I shouldn't think that anyone would care to get anything straight from that source. No more than what comes "out of the mouths of babes and sucklings" which is too distressing even to think about.

This is becoming rather unpleasant. I think I'll give up trying to master any more modish words and phrases and content myself with my simple two-syllable vocabulary.

. . . with my school middy blouse . . .

Have You Heard about My Vacation?

Anybody who has just returned from a vacation . . . particularly a vacation in a distant land, lives for a time in a little world of his own. Nothing seems real . . . the fact that he's home, the fact that he has actually been in the distant land and, above all, the fact that every person he encounters isn't dying to hear a detailed account of his trip. At the present time, I am in a happy state of having just returned from Japan. It is a happy state for me at any rate, although I'm not sure that the happiness is shared by my friends, for I've noticed a certain bracing of their shoulders when we meet for the first time since my return and they realize that they're cornered and are going to have to ask me about my trip. Actually it strikes me as quite incredible that they don't ask me about it right off. Just this morning as I drove out of my gate I all but ran headlong into my next-door neighbor coming out of his own driveway. We slammed on respective brakes, paused to wave and exchange blithe apologies and to my wounded surprise he never for a moment said, "I hear you're just back from Japan." The only reason he didn't hear it then and there was due to the fact that I had heard that he was just back from Scotland and, not feeling up to a panegyrical summary of the beauties of the Hebrides, I hurried off before he could get started. I still, however, think it was curiously unneighborly of him not to have asked me about Japan.

For at present I can't resist the impulse to talk about Japan at the drop of a hat, even if people are meticulously careful not to drop any hats, and even if I know perfectly well that the last thing in the world anybody wants to hear is a detailed account of anybody else's holiday safari. The reaction of every listener who is accosted with one of these gratuitous travelogues is the same. To begin with, he doesn't listen; then, as soon as it's humanly possible, he changes the subject, and what he changes it to is a second gratuitous travelogue describing his own recent holiday. Only last week, a lady friend whom I ran across on the commuters' train felt duty-bound to inquire politely, if somewhat halfheartedly, "How was Japan?" and as I drew a deep breath before starting to tell her, she started in telling me how Sweden was. Sweden lasted all the way to Syosset and, since she was due to get off the train at Cold Spring Harbor, the Rising Sun of Japan barely got above the Long Island tracks.

There is another and more insidious type of listener, and that is the travel snob who lets you get going and for a time appears to be paying rapt attention to your every word, then ruins your act when he suddenly indicates a prior and superior familiarity with the country you're describing by dropping the name of some oh-so-native restaurant or some obscure little shop and adding with smiling condescension, "You went there often *of course*," and of *course* you never went there once.

It is an abominable trait, this last, and one which I have to a degree. In all honesty I admit to all these deplorable failings, those of the irrepressible tourist and those of his reluctant audience. Curious the compulsion which makes one keep on, quite consciously, being a crashing bore. It isn't that we all haven't time and again encountered the horrid example who buttonholes us for hours in order to give a blow-by-blow description of his trip without allowing us one moment to retaliate with a description of ours. One friend of mine has made me feel I never want to see Venice again, another has persuaded me to strike Brazil off my list and only last summer, coming back on the ship, I shared a table with a couple who should be reported to the Hawaiian Chamber of Commerce as sabotaging tourist trade in the Islands. At every meal, all the way across the Pacific, no topic came up which didn't in some way lead them straight back to Oahu. They kept saying "Aloha" on all occasions, in place of "Good morning," "Good night" and "Here's mud in your eye!" Their conversation fairly reeked of pineapple and leis, with an accompaniment of steel guitars and interspersed with a lot of words which it's doubtful if even Queen Liliuokalani ever knew. When the boat stopped for the day in Honolulu, I could hardly bring myself to go ashore. They drove me into making a daily vow to the waves, which was . . . "When I get back home, I will *not* talk about Japan!" . . . then, not to commit myself too far I *did* add, ". . . unless, of course, the subject comes up in conversation."

It is frustrating to discover how seldom the subject of Japan does come up in conversation. People don't just throw out helpful openers like "What *is* the name of those sliding doors you see on Japanese houses?" or "I'd so love to have someone tell me what Kyoto is like in festival time." Now and then the subject is brought up obliquely by some unsuspecting victim who instantly becomes a captive audience, like the taxi-driver the other day who came out, in complete innocence, with "Have you ever seen worse traffic?" and quick as a flash I had him with "Yes! In Tokyo." At this the poor devil felt obliged to rejoin "Yeah? Is that bad?" It took the distance of Sixty-sixth Street to Penn Station to tell him just how bad. At all events, the good man got an extra tip.

Failing such golden opportunities, the alternative is to depend upon native ingenuity to bring up the subject. One can't be like the man who was so dying to tell a joke concerning some firearms he finally, in desperation, cracked a spoon down on the table and said "BANG! Speaking of guns . . . " In other words, it's unconvincing when the company present is discussing a certain film to come out with "I haven't seen it because I've been in the Orient." While drinking a cup of tea, one can't very well start an unsolicited account of the Tea Ceremony. And it's a bit weak to employ the interjection method such as "Funny, a man was saying that very same thing only the other day over in Kamakura" because the chances are that not everyone knows the locale of Kamakura and that what the man was saying may have had nothing whatsoever to do with either Kamakura or Japan and that no one is going to say "Why, were you there? Do tell us about it!" and there you are left wondering how you're ever going to get around to giving forth with that anecdote about the time you got all fouled up with the chopsticks and shot the rice into your host's lap. I've waited days for someone to bring up the recent Russo-Japanese conference so that I could casually drop "Oh yes, I met Mr. Shigemitsu last summer in Tokyo." The nearest I've succeeded lately was to maneuver one person into talking about lawns and from

there I raised the problem of the Japanese beetle.
But before I could launch with any logical grace
into a short dissertation regarding the country
of their origin, some oaf had switched things
into an animated causerie concerning the mat-
ing habits of the mud wasp, and this naturally
led to a reappraisal of the Kinsey report, after
which, who on earth wanted to hear me give
my trip-to-Japan report?

For I am not one of those fabulous wits of
the civilized salon who can steer a conversation
into channels no matter how remote they may
be from the subject under discussion. I was especially aware of this deficiency two years ago
after I had had the privilege of dining with the
Dowager Queen of England at the time of her
visit to New York. Naturally I was dying to
tell everybody about it, but how to bring it up?
I had just returned from Hollywood and had
had to listen to too many name droppers of the
"as-I-was-telling-Louis-B.-Mayer" variety to stoop
to anything like ". . . someone was saying the
other evening . . . . who *was* it! . . . oh I know,
it was Queen Elizabeth! . . . well, she was saying
. . . " I would try to direct every verbal inter-
change into any topic . . . England, the Cunard
Line, even Elizabeth, New Jersey . . . any excuse

for me to come out modestly with "Funny your mentioning Queen Elizabeth. I happened to have been dining with Her Majesty last week." But as I could never swing it, I'd eventually give up and just say blatantly and apropos of nothing, "Guess whom I had dinner with last week?"

In the case of the returned voyager, one way to bring up the topic of his trip is through the use of props. Especially in the home. Eyecatchers in the way of bright-colored brochures or a few illustrated magazines printed in the language of the recently visited country can come in handy if left lying about with carefully planned carelessness. I am, to the distress of my household, still in the loot-displaying stage. Being the sweetheart of the souvenir-shop keeper the world over, I return from any foreign travel laden with a welter of artsy-craftsy objects which, to be sure, may often as not be found in duplicate right down the street in Bloomingdale's basement, but then it's so much more fun and trouble to lug them back from overseas. At the present time, little Oriental artifacts clutter every surface of my house. A Japanese matchbox reposes in every ashtray . . . which is also Japanese (the Italian ones being put aside until after my next trip to the Mediterranean). Guests who have drinks are obliged to set down their glasses on lacquer coasters and spread over their laps quaint finger napkins "which," I explain as I hand them out, "are of course the sort of thing you'll find in your geisha house," Why I should feel compelled to call it "*your* geisha house" I wouldn't know, except that it sounds more authoritative . . . and of course I take care to pronounce it "gay-sha" just as I admit I'm calling the traditional garment a "*kee*-mo-noh." Not everyone rises to the bait, although now and then some patient soul will with resignation sigh and say "Well, *tell* us about *our* geisha houses" and I'm off in a cloud of cherry blossoms.

Further, by way of props, are those items of native costuming in which the returned voyager can't resist getting herself all rigged up . . . . the coolie coats from Hong Kong, the Arab bracelets from Algiers, the huaraches from Acapulco. It's an understandable weakness, to me at any rate, for I've had it most of my life . . . ever since at the age of fifteen I was taken on a tour through Spain and was so impressed with the distinction, all the ensuing fall I wore an immense tortoise-shell comb and long red earrings along with my school middy blouse. I've been back from the Orient now for three weeks, but I'm

still going about decked in bits and pieces of
Old Nippon. I don't quite saunter down Park
Avenue twirling a paper umbrella and I don't
idly finger a double strand of Mikimoto pearls
. . . . only because I wasn't able to afford the
latter. But I *am* apt to feign feeling chilly on
what may be a stiflingly hot evening and go to
fetch my jacket of Imperial brocade and I have
been guilty of coming down for supper in a
pair of white cotton *tabi* socks and slippers with a
thong down the middle "because they're so comfortable" . . . . which of course is a lie. For
unless one is blessed with widely splayed toes,
this footgear can in no time become a form
of exquisite torture. Such little Cho-Cho San
displays don't always produce the desired effect.
Not everyone on seeing them exclaims, "Wherever
did you find *that* lovely thing?" and once when
I casually opened out a small fan (it was made of
carved sandalwood and produced not the slightest breeze whatsoever) everyone looked hastily
in the other direction.

For a time I carried a ten-yen bill in my purse
(along with that silver dollar I keep handy in
case I feel an overwhelming urge to talk about
Nevada). It proved a pretty good conversation
piece when I'd start to hand it out, then in

pretty confusion retract it saying, "Look at me, giving you ten yen!" or "Mercy! I can't seem to get rid of my Japanese currency!" The conversation didn't always get going, particularly when the person on the other end didn't know a yen from a Confederate dollar and cared less.

The one tedium I have spared my friends and family is having to inspect examples of amateur photography. When the modern camera, with its multiple devices which require a degree in navigation to master, superseded the dear old box Brownie, I gave up compiling any further "My Vacation" albums. And I haven't had the heart to try a three-dimensional color camera. I've spent too many hours in the houses of my friends, painfully squinting into awkward stereopticon contraptions while whoever took the shots hovers fatuously above asking, "What are you looking at now?" snatches out the slide, says, "Oh yes, that's the Forum," then replaces it upside down.

Maybe the problem of the irrepressible tourist could be solved by the company which has made out so well with the telephone Answering Service. They might go further and set up a Listening Service, for the benefit both of the returned tourist who feels he can't bear it if he doesn't talk about his trip and of his friends who know they can't bear it if he does. Some sort of receiving instrument in the form of a box, attractively finished in optional period style to go with all types of furniture, might be installed in a quiet corner of every living room and when the craving to talk reached dope-addiction proportions, the device could be turned on and the sufferer led gently over to unburden his soul to a sympathetic voice which would make appropriate response while the rest of the company could go back to the television set.

As a matter of fact, such Listening Service might come in handy for any number of other emergencies. If someone were to say "Have you heard about my operation?" the answer would be "Yes, but the folks on Listening Service haven't." Then there are those people on diets who could count their calories to the sympathetic voice, and golfers who could relate their scores and never even detect a yawn from the other end. Husbands might find it useful when their wives can't resist giving forth with a report of their bridge club meeting and wives would undoubtedly find it invaluable when their husbands insist upon explaining an involved scientific process.

I offer this as a revolutionary suggestion. All I ask is a generous percentage of the profits.

. . . propped on my hero's shoulder . . .

On Being
Outsized

When I was in my mid-teens I read a novel about a beautiful Titian-haired creature who lived on a vast estate near the Kimberly mines. She was madly adored by a devastatingly handsome overseer who wore polo clothes and a pith helmet and whenever he came to call on her, he leapt onto the veranda with a single bound, lifted her from the hammock in which she was languidly swinging and, breathing through dilated nostrils, planted a lingering kiss on her brow. I found this all quite beautiful and my ambition was to be just like the Titian-haired creature and have a young man on the order of the handsome overseer spring at me and kiss me on the brow. There wasn't much I could do about whipping up an African setting, but I did give my hair a henna rinse which turned it less Titian red than El Greco green. As for the young man, I was not too particular. He didn't have to wear polo clothes and I certainly would not have demanded a pith helmet. He simply had to be handsome . . . if possible . . . and above all things able to kiss me on the brow.

For at that gangly period I was known as the Tall Girl of my set and the few callow youths who "dated" me would hardly have been able to let linger a kiss on any feature much above my chin. That is, if we were to try it sitting. If a bull's-eye more romantically satisfactory than the chin were effected, it had to be from a seated vantage point . . . and it still was never the brow . . . . even if I thrust it forward in the manner of an amorous heifer.

American girls in those pre-vitamin days were not the Amazons many of them are now, but

I by fifteen had shot up to my present height
of five feet seven, which though not extraordi-
nary now was, at the start of the twenties, practically a deformity. I tried to disguise it as desperately as I tried to conceal the bands on my
teeth. The latter disgrace could be kept from
view, when I thought of it, by an expression of
mysterious sultriness which I hoped was a dead
ringer for Clara Kimball Young, and, if laugh-
ter were inevitable, by a hand held across the
mouth in the manner of the "speak no evil"
monkey. Reducing my height was a more complex matter. At that period girls did not go
about in flat shoes, espadrilles and those depressing products of Greenwich Village, black sneakers
and black ribbed stockings. Nor would any Junior
Miss have been found dead attending a dance in
ballet slippers. High heels were THE thing and
if a despairing mother protested that "they'll
ruin your feet for life!" some well-contrived
nagging on the part of the daughter could bring
about a compromise in the way of Cuban heels.
But even these added a couple of inches to a
girl's height. As long as one stood still the problem could be partially solved by assuming the
pose in which Mrs. Vernon Castle's photographs
were taken . . . a willowy stance with hands

clasped in the vague region of the thigh bone, one leg bent, the other trailing off to one side with ankle elegantly dislocated, an example of human distortion recently resuscitated in the musical show *The Boy Friend*. There was also a frightfully chic posture known as the "debutante slouch," a pose of deliberate imbecility and impending collapse, immortalized in the drawings of John Held, Jr. (I once overheard a friend of Mother's describing me as "Poor Mrs. Skinner's daughter . . . the girl who looks like a croquet wicket.") But for all these subterfuges there came the moment when one had to walk down a street or into a room with a boy. And there was the further and for me more desperate moment when I had to dance, for most of my partners were shorter than I.

My dream was to be asked to a Yale, Harvard or Princeton prom by a football hero, big, bold, brainless and beautiful. The only proms I ever attended were ones at Penn State, Haverford and Hill School and the youths who asked me were serious, spectacled, short and, what added to humiliation, scholarly. One of them *was* a champion, to be sure, but I didn't boast much as to the nature of his triumphs, for his championship was in chess. He kept solemnly

winning at intercollegiate tournaments of that
royal game and why he should have taken a fancy
to a girl who couldn't even win at a game of
parcheesi, I shall never know. The mortifica-
tion of his being a chess champion might have
been overcome, if only he had been taller than
I . . . or even of the same height. That was the
dawn of "cheek to cheek" dancing, a daring innovation which shocked our parents and filled
us with rapture not unmixed with perspiration.
In the case of the chess champion, our dancing
was less cheek-to-cheek than temple-to-jowl
and I needn't state whose was the jowl. I tried
to mend matters by dancing with bent knees,
which didn't look so well, or putting myself into
a sharp incline with chin propped on my hero's
shoulder to steady me. At least we took up a
good deal of space as we'd twirl to the strains
of "April Showers" while with wistful eye I'd
observe the passing couples, the huge athlete
gods with their partners, each a giddy little
midget with fluffy head barely reaching the altitude of a brawny chest.

This was about the time when adolescent
America hit upon the "line," an exchange of
verbal inanities. One popular and somewhat
"fast" cliché was for a girl to look up at her

partner and murmur "My, you're so big and strong!" and the rejoinder, "But oh so gentle!" Had my chess champion and I engaged in this verbal passage-at-arms, the speeches would have had to have been reversed.

I soon forewent the joys of prom-trotting to go on the stage. Here I continued inwardly to bewail my height, for most actors are fairly short men (my own father was a good two inches shorter than I). My height, however, turned out to be an asset, not so much to me as to certain comedians who deliberately scored off it. What jobs I was able to find were in a number of mild little comedies, most of them immediate failures. My roles were hardly distinguished. I was usually cast as the leading lady's unpleasant sister or a snooty neighbor, characters having little to do with the play other than to appear at the rise of the curtain while the audience was still being seated, utter a few banalities, then, on the entrance of the more important members of the cast, to exit and reappear only during moments which needed filling in. Mine were less theatrical appearances than a series of disappearances.

In Booth Tarkington's lightweight but charming play *Tweedles* I played a rich widow (grass) who kept making bold but unsuccessful advances to the youthful hero (Gregory Kelly) by trying once in each act to entice him to come for a ride in my roadster (a Stutz Bearcat). This might have been a pretty dashing part if I hadn't gone by the unfortunate name of Mrs. Ricketts and if every time I made overtures to Gregory Kelly who was a good five inches shorter than I, he hadn't convulsed the audience by slowly lifting his gaze upward in bewilderment and dread as though a lady stilt-walker had coyly proposed "Shall we dance?" Ruth Gordon (then Mrs. Gregory Kelly) played the heroine. She too was extremely short (she still is) and during my scenes with the minute pair, they pulled off a lot of side-splitting stage business which added to my giantess complex.

Ruth at that time was zestfully taking up numerous endeavors for the sake of her art. One of her more inspired enthusiasms was ballet dancing. A ballet master named Kosloff had a school somewhere near Carnegie Hall and Ruth talked me into joining her in a beginner's class. She said such training would make us better actresses. I had protested that I didn't know the first thing about dancing and was sure to fall flat, but she said pooh that was nothing, she fell flat all the time. I was soon to learn that when Ruth fell, she hadn't so far to go, nor did she shake the foundations of the floor. Hers was like the graceful bending of the reed as compared with the crash of the mighty oak.

The class was made up of professional dancers and talented apprentices. There were also one or two luminaries from musical shows. I remember staring open-jawed at Louise Groody as she stood on one toe and lifted her other foot high above her head. Conditioned by the paintings of Degas, I had expected all ballet pupils to be dressed in filmy tutus. But not these coryphees. They wore little romper numbers of gingham, halter tops and abbreviated bloomers in which, actually, they looked quite cute. These practice outfits were to be procured from a theatrical supply store on Broadway and I bought the largest size they carried. It was a pink and white check and in it I looked rather like Fanny Brice as Baby Snooks.

Why Maestro Kosloff admitted me to the class I can't imagine, except that those were the years when Grand Dukes were driving taxicabs and Russians would endure many horrors in order to gain a livelihood. It was all too apparent that the great man took a dim view of me. To

make the view even dimmer he kept me behind the back row when the class was lined up
for elementary steps and positions. What the
steps and positions were, I could not have told
anyone, for the maestro's accent was such that
he might have been giving instructions to Nijin-
sky in their native tongue. The rest of the class,
through some aesthetic receptivity, were able
to get his meaning . . . all except Ruth, but she
was little and graceful and nobody noticed her.
Everyone, on the other hand, noticed me. Particularly myself. For the walls were solidly mir-
rored and there was no avoiding the myriad
horrid reflections.

I soon gave up any attempt at interpreting
Kosloff's spoken directions and just tried to ape
the movements of the dancer in front of me
. . . all, that is, except the trick of standing
on my toes. I made up for that in pantomime
session by occasionally standing on the toes of
others. When time came for the dreaded bar
exercises, I was shunted off to the far end of
that traditional pole. Although my legs were
the longest in the room, I actually took up
very little space owing to the fact that I could
never lift a leg up onto the bar unless my knee
was well bent, and a bent leg in ballet danc-

ing is as serious a flagrancy as a bent ankle in figure skating. The bar was about the height of my lower ribs and neither leg when straightened would, of its own momentum, come up any higher than the calf of the other.

During bar practice the master would go from one pupil to the next giving each the benefit of his individual instruction. He never wasted any time on me other than to tell me with a shudder to "joost kip on tryink." One day, however, he could bear the sight of my giraffelike struggles no longer and sharply ordering me to keep my leg rigid "even if it *keels* you!" seized my ankle and, breathing like a lumberman lifting a stubborn log, managed to foist my foot up onto the bar. The pain was intense. For both of us, I imagine. I endured mine, stoically thinking how all this was going to make me a better actress. Kosloff gasped out a triumphant "There! You see?" I gasped back that yes, I saw, and what happened next everybody else saw too. This was the sudden departure of my other foot from off the floor and the hurtling collapse of my body in a catapult which felled us both. I shrieked a hysterical "oops!" and laughed lamely. The maestro did not laugh. He gathered up his dignity and self and coldly ordered the spellbound pupils to continue their exercises. At the finish of the hour he called me aside and told me, more in sorrow than in anger, that God had not intended me to be a ballerina. I bowed to his and God's decision and resigned from the class. The following week I signed up at Arthur Murray's and learned the Charleston at which, if I must say so, I became quite expert.

Mine was an average quota of beaux and . . . need I announce it? . . . most of them were shorter than I. My most faithful swain was a pint-sized lad who had a job with a travel agency. He could talk impressively about Rome, Cairo, Buenos Aires and Java (he'd never been to any of those places). He also was a Charleston enthusiast. The two of us cut an interesting figure in the moderate-priced night-clubs we frequented. To be sure, from a rear view, I might occasionally have given the impression that I was dancing alone, but what cared I? I did manage to hook one admirer who was rangy, handsome and startlingly tall. The day he called me "Little One" and kissed me on the brow, I got engaged to him. But it wasn't a long engagement. He was a Greenwich Village "bohemian" who wore corduroy jackets and talked about Picasso and Stravinsky. He had an aversion for any form of chair and all that glorious height was squandered as he sprawled on the floor at my feet, reading aloud his completely incomprehensible poetry.

During the ensuing years I gradually stopped thinking of myself. Not that I shrank in any way, but that the people with whom I associated seemed to become taller. I married a tall man and gave birth to a son who has been obliging enough now to measure six feet four inches.

It was only during a recent trip to Japan that my former giantess complex came rushing back to cramp my spirit if not my stature. That same six-feet-four-inch son, then in the Navy and stationed in the Far East, has given a depressing picture of the American female tourist as she makes an ecstatically appreciative entrance into an exquisite little geisha house or delicate Nipponese tearoom. "In she stalks," he said, "the Statue of Liberty dressed by Peck and Peck." And this was pretty much the way I felt in that land of charm, beauty and tiny, graceful people.

In Japan there is a great deal of bending to be done. The younger generation of the children of the Rising Sun may be growing taller, but the traditional architecture remains the same and an average Japanese door is of a height suitable

for no adult American with the possible exception
of some of our jockeys. One of the first things
to learn in Japan is how to duck. Then there's a
lot of bending to be done in regard to the social amenities. I am thinking specifically of the
formal bow. Before going to the Land of Flow-
ers I had always dismissed its ceremonious bow
as something to be seen only in a third-rate pro-
duction of *The Mikado*. But I was to discover that
the formal bow is real and ever present. The Japanese are always bowing. They bow when they
meet. They bow when they say goodbye, they
bow when they pay one another compliments, or
when they admire a garden or when someone
makes a witty remark or sends honorable regards
to someone's honorable family. They bow when
they exchange cards . . . and they're constantly
exchanging cards. And after they've had a group
photograph taken (which is another thing they do
a lot) they bow to each other and to the photogra-
pher. It would not surprise me to learn that after
a tooth extraction, the patient leaps from the
chair to exchange bows of smiling relief with the
dentist. A woman is supposed to make a deeper
bow than a man and to outnumber him with a few
extra ones after he stops. The visiting female
from America is regarded as being exempt from

these elaborate civilities. However, mine has always been the fatuous travel policy that when in Rome do as the tourist overacting a Roman does, and right from the start I went in for the formal bow with bright enthusiasm. The brightness was rather dimmed by that same son who after watching me greet an exquisite little geisha told me I'd better not try any more, I only appeared to be doing waist-reducing exercises.

There is nothing like Japanese food and the observances in regard to consuming it to give one a Gulliver-in-Lilliput complex. There is the formal dinner . . . the sort where everyone sits on the floor around a low table, where endless delicious and mysterious courses are served in delicate lacquer bowls and where the sole eating implements for everything from raw fish to clear soup are a single pair or chopsticks, which in my case might as well have been a a pair of soda fountain straws.

The most nerve-racking aspect of the Japanese meal is that all the time an enchanting little serving lady in bright kimono kneels beside you watching your every mouthful . . . that is, those you've succeeded in getting *into* your mouth and, in my case, mopping up the ones scattered onto my tray. Everything connected with a Japanese meal is dainty. The lids of the lacquer bowls are so light, in removing one quickly you are likely to toss it back over your shoulder. *Sake,* the native rice wine, is served in a microscopic porcelain cup so fragile, it's like drinking from a robin's egg. The little serving creature keeps offering to replenish it with hot *sake* which she pours from a tiny vase while you gingerly hold forth your cup, taking pains not to crush it.

Japanese mealtime complications for the foreigner are not limited to what takes place above the table. It is what takes below, in the way of constant limb adjustment, that gives one the appearance of a polite but restless Gargantua. An Eastern lady can kneel gracefully on a cushion throughout a three-hour meal and never twitch a muscle. Not so her Western sister. I would start out demurely kneeling and be able to stay that way for a scant ten minutes. Then I'd flop into a sidesaddle position and be able to last that way as long as fifteen minutes when violent cramps would necessitate a flop onto the other sidesaddle for another quarter of an hour. At the end of which time I'd heave myself into the attitude of the seated Buddha . . . not that I had much of that deity's serene dignity, especially when once I made the error of wearing a narrow skirt. Sometimes my knees would come up sharply under the low table and raise it with a jarring flip. My most consoling moment was when an American expatriate who has lived so long in this delectable land he rather fancies himself a latter-day Lafcadio Hearn sat opposite me and I noted that he too was doing a considerable bit of surreptitious squirming about. When, therefore, his foot shot out under the low table and landed in my lap, I was so pleased I almost shook it.

After every meal or tea ceremony there comes the moment of getting back onto one's stockinged feet . . . all shoes having of course been left outside. The Japanese woman has an acrobatic skill which enables her to rise straight up from the kneeling position in a single beautiful swooping movement without lurching forward, without boosting herself by shoving down with hand on the floor, without even grunting. The less agile American charmer, in trying to get herself erect, reverts momentarily to the ape and scuttles about on all fours until she finds some lever like a chair or table leg with which to haul herself up.

If Japan is a country in which one finds oneself committing well-intended gaucheries, its charming people, who are the most polite and considerate in the world, are ever ready to tide one across awkward moments. I recall a moment in Kyoto when, on entering the Ni-Jo Palace, I all but scalped myself while walking through a low doorway. "Oh dear!" I moaned to no one in particular, "I feel so *huge* in this country!" The little guide who was conducting us smiled with humorous understanding and said, "Imagine, madame, how *we* feel in yours!" Somehow I had never thought of that. The victim of the giant-complex may take comfort in the realization that maybe there are some people who suffer from a pygmy one.

. . . that pint I always smuggle onto a plane . . .

Idle
in Idlewild

To be obliged to wait about in an overcrowded railroad station is a depressing experience. To await the late departure of a plane in a jammed-up airport is a worse one. And when that airport is Idlewild at the height of the rush hours, that experience takes on nightmare proportions. I know whereof I speak, for I recently endured the

Note: This article was written before the new installations were put up at our International Airport, but the sentiment still holds good.

torture of being held up for the better part of four hours in the ghastly confines of our International Air Terminal. I was booked for a flight to California. To be sure I had checked over the phone before leaving home and to be sure that voice wreathed in smiles had said that my plane was expected to leave on schedule and, in tones of splendid cheer, had thanked me so much for calling.

I arrived at Idlewild, went to the proper counter, weighed in my luggage and handed my ticket to one of those comely young men who look like movie actors playing pilots. It was only then that he informed me, that in regard to my take-off there would be a "slight delay." He too spoke in tones of splendid cheer. When I asked how slight and why, he smiled tactfully and said that at the moment he didn't know, but that it would be announced shortly. He was still splendid but somewhat less cheery and it all struck me as ominous.

The behavior of these discreet employees behind airline counters is distressingly remindful of the subtle tactics of nurses in hospitals. A well-trained clerk is as loath to come clean and give the apprehensive passenger the real lowdown on what is causing a flight delay as a nurse

is to tell the patient the actual degree of his
temperature. Passenger and patient alike are
treated as fractious children incapable of facing
the truth, and that's no way in which to treat
anyone cursed with an overvivid imagination.
When a nurse, snatching a thermometer from
my fevered lips and studying it well beyond my
reach, smiles soothingly and coos that it's "just
a leedle bit up" I instantly conclude that up is
somewhere in the vicinity of 105°, and when an
airline official says that there will be a delay
owing to "a minor mechanical difficulty" I assume that the difficulty is nothing less minor
than the discovery that all four engines are
loose and likely to fall out just as we gain our
altitude.

The delay on this recent occasion was due to
"a weather condition." Even this explanation
was offered with veiled discretion, as though the
"condition" were of a delicate nature and one
to be mentioned only with lowered eyes. To
have stated with honest candor that it was simply a matter of fog would have been, perhaps,
a violation of airline code. For fog it was . . .
thick, wooly, drifting fog. Anybody could have
told you that. Anybody, that is, who could look
out a window and realize the horrid fact that

the control tower was blanketed in slathers of ceiling zero.

I asked the comely young man how long he thought I'd have to wait. He was too well bred to answer "Have you any more jokes to tell me, lady?" Instead he said that it might be an hour, maybe less, maybe longer as the "equipment" hadn't been able to "get through" . . . whatever that meant . . . and by way of a sort of consolation prize handed me a slip of paper which, it appeared, enabled me to get a free meal at the Brass Rail Restaurant. It seems to be a facet of airline psychology that the one way of soothing the disgruntled patron is to feed him, no matter what the time of day or night. It was then 11 A.M. I had just consumed a large breakfast at home. The thought of a meal, even one on the company, was gagging.

I decided to wait nearby for further news and looked about for a place in which to sit down. Against the opposing wall were six seats overflowing with seven persons, in addition to a baby and a poodle. I should have remembered that few airports provide sufficient resting places in the immediate vicinity of their check-in counters. Maybe this is to give the impression that the aeronautic mode of transportation is so

swiftly efficient there is no time between de-
scent from bus to boarding of plane to waste
on any such decadent nonsense as taking it easy.
Over the years the authorities of other airports
throughout the country, realizing that punctuality
is not invariably the rule for plane schedules,
have given compassionate thought to the comfort of the waiting traveler. I have spent many
pleasant interludes relaxing in the sit-downeries
of the Boston, Washington and Chicago ter-
minals. Try, on the other hand, to relax at Idlewild (or at La Guardia too for that matter) during
the rush hour or when a "weather condition"
has held up several major flights. Every one
of the totally insufficient number of seats throughout the building will have been appropriated and
there is nothing to do but stand still or wander about.

To wander about was no fun that day. Neither
was standing still any treat, for there was no es-
caping the moiling mob. Mine was not the only
delayed flight and several hundred extra voy-
agers, humid and hectic, were jamming the clam-
orous lobbies or hallways or whatever you choose
to call those dismal connecting boxcars which
comprise our International Air Terminal. The
prevailing atmosphere was one of panic, as

though war had been declared and a desperate
populace were trying to evacuate itself. Retarded
passengers were rushing from counters to phone-
booths and back to counters again, incoming
passengers were rushing to find where to claim
their luggage, people who had come to meet
other people were rushing to locate them, the
rest, catching the spirit of things, were just rushing. Scattered among those unhappy inmates who
had of necessity to be caged for a time in this
madhouse were a few dawdling onlookers, sim-
ple-minded citizens who had brought Sonny and
Cissie out to see the big airplanes and had
now come in to gape at these frenzied itinerants
with the morbid fascination of 18th century Lon-
doners watching the antics at Bedlam.

In the midst of such hurly-burly, there wasn't
even the solace I knew of old in crowded railroad stations of perching on my luggage. That
impedimenta adorned with cabalistic tags sig-
nifying Los Angeles had long since disappeared
on a moving belt into a maw of oblivion. The
small canvas bag I was carrying by hand could
hardly be perched upon. Even if I were to try
it, the result would be a crash of shattered glass
and the irreparable loss of that pint I always
smuggle onto a plane in case unusually fright-

ful weather prevails or an engine starts belching flames.

The comely young man was telling everyone not to leave the premises as the fog might lift any minute and that incoming equipment arrive. There was nothing to do but wait. I set forth in search of a place in which to sit and for the next three and a half hours was to continue to do nothing but search. Every seat was occupied by someone who had got there first and was clinging to it with the defiance of a gold prospector staking out a claim. Surely, I thought, someone would eventually get up. Either no one ever did or some other seat searcher got there ahead of me. Heartless oafs, they appeared to be settled there for whatever would be the duration. A few of them didn't even look like prospective passengers. A group of small boys in baseball caps who had taken over all the seats opposite Iberia Airlines were certainly not bound for Spain, while three louts sprawling on a bench near Sabena seemed to have settled there for the sole purpose of eating a prolonged picnic lunch.

At the foot of the stairs leading to the Observation Deck is a large window on whose low, narrow sill I squatted for a time. There were four additional squatters. They were apparently

South or Central Americans from one of those indeterminate countries one knew when one was a child and played Flags. They were each very large and very moist and they all talked at once in clacking, excitable Spanish, sounding like feeding hour in a parrot house.

Their voices played interesting counterpoint with the overall din. In addition to the re-echoing noises of the mob came the continual rasping cacophony of the loudspeaker. For a time its announcements sounded romantically adventuresome. The fog had not daunted some planes, for Air France was requesting *messieurs les passagers* to get *à bord pour* Paris while the Venezuelan Airlines were asking their *passajeros* to do likewise *para* Caracas, while KLM was telling the world of the imminent arrival of The Flying Dutchman. BOAC in impeccable English was loading the Monarch for London while our native lines in more peccable American were clarioning out advices about Rome, Tokyo and Miami. In between these colorful outbursts came those startling demands that Mr. Whatsis come immediately to the United Airlines desk and that a Mrs. Whoozis report forthwith to Pan American. There is something almost indecent about these blaring summonses. It is as though Mr. Whatsis or Mrs. Whoozis had been guilty of some grave misdemeanor and upon turning up before their respective desks would face an aeronautic tribunal and a severe dressing down. During my long hours of waiting, a Dr. Krantz was periodically summoned to report to Swissair. As far as I could make out, Dr. Krantz never got up the nerve to appear.

After twenty minutes of squatting with bent back on the low window sill, my muscles became so cramped I was afraid they'd get set and I'd have to board the plane in a Toulouse-Lautrec posture. I straightened myself out and returned to the counter where there was still no news of that incoming equipment and the advice was still not to leave the premises. I had as yet no trace of appetite, but that meal at the Brass Rail struck me as a means both of killing time and of sitting down. It turned out that scores of others had been similarly struck. Every table was jammed and the waiting line looked like the queue outside the first showings of *Gone With the Wind*. (I'd like to state here parenthetically and by way of further complaint that with the exception of a small oyster bar, an equally small sandwich counter and a

snackery on the Observation Deck, the Brass
Rail seems to be Idlewild's only restaurant, and
while a wildly busy staff do an amazingly efficient turnover job, to undertake the provender
demands of the thousands of persons who flock
through our terminal is about as adequate as four
Good Humor men undertaking the feeding of
a regiment.)

The restaurant portion of the Brass Rail was
fairly giving at the seams. I saw, however, to
my surprise and delight that the bar section was
practically empty. Babbling soft apologies I
slithered through the waiting line and plopped
down at a small table. A waitress lady came up
to inform me that it was Sunday. The bar section didn't open till one. It was then a minute
before noon. My expression must have roused
her compassion, for she bent over to tell me
in the whisper of a stage conspirator that she
could bring me a sandwich and a cup of coffee
. . . she wasn't supposed to . . . but she could, just
bring me that. I wanted no coffee and I hate
sandwiches in every known variety of the loathe-
some concoction, but it seemed ungrateful not
to take advantage of this friendly smuggler's benevolent offer. Besides, I could hardly sit there
without some sort of plausible prop so I let her

slip me a cheese on rye part of which I was able to get down my throat by dint of easy shoves.

Such killing of time was but a partial death, for a clock pointed to twelve-twenty. It would have been restful to have kept on sitting there till the bar opened . . . and perhaps to have stayed on a bit after that cheering event. But by now the overflow from the restaurant had started to move in and had taken possession of the remaining free tables. Everyone who was standing in the waiting line was glaring at everyone who was seated with expressions which distinctly said "PIGS!" I meekly paid my check (a sandwich didn't seem worth charging to the line) and reluctantly left this air-conditioned respite for the heat-unconditioned maelstrom of the terminal. Needless to report that there were still no available seats, so I again took up that slow and aimless strolling. At one time I thought to change this to a brisk and purposeful walk in the fresh air and went outside the building. But the air wasn't particularly fresh that day and the narrow sidewalk cluttered with baggage, skycaps and bus passengers offered no space for a constitutional. The only other hiking grounds lay amid the serried cars of the parking lot.

I went back into the overpopulated hell of

the inner terminal. My feet were hurting, my legs felt as though they'd been filled with lead and there was of course not a vacant seat within sight. I drifted past a shoeshine stand noting that there was one unoccupied chair. The shoes I had on were patent leather strap sandals and I didn't think I'd be allowed to go in and just sit down even if I paid the price of a shine which couldn't be had. A sign saying SHELTER had an inviting look. I wondered if to follow in the direction indicated by the arrow would lead to a cozy cellar where for half an hour one might stretch out quietly on the floor. But it seemed doubtful if plane departures would be announced in air-raid shelters. I might, I speculated, slump down in the spacious comfort of a telephone booth and rest there for a while pretending, if need be, to be making a great number of urgent calls. Every booth, however, was taken and the sight of all the impatient people waiting to get an empty one made me realize the move would hardly be popular. There were, of course, those places of retreat, clearly indicated in three languages, the last word being *mujeres,* although they were hardly the happiest of solutions. I looked longingly in at a barbershop where members of the pampered sex were voluptuously lolling back for the happily drawn-out interim of shave, haircut and whatever goes on under those hot face towels. There was a closely packed sandwich counter onto one of whose stools I might eventually have squeezed myself, but the thought of facing another sandwich was not to be borne. Then there was a little booth in which one could sit for the privilege of taking one's own photograph and awaiting its development and delivery. But the whole process was advertised as taking in all fifty seconds and this didn't seem worth a quarter. What was more, I would have felt obligated to look at the picture.

Near a luggage station I spotted a folding wheel chair and approached it surreptitiously only to discover it to be padlocked and chained to the wall. To hire it would have meant also hiring someone to push me about in it and to convince anyone I needed such emergency service would have required some convincing evidence like crutches.

I plodded on forlorn as a refugee seeking any sort of haven. There isn't much visual diversion at Idlewild. Certain airlines have murals of world maps, if you want to brush up on your geography, and on the walls of Swissair are some nice blowups of Switzerland. Window shopping is restricted to a scattering of establishments in one of which one can stare for a time at men's shirts, in another, at women's stockings. All the other emporia specialize in camera equipment and cutlery, especially cutlery. Why it is assumed that the traveler should wish to carry with him photographic paraphernalia is easily understood. But why he should want to stock up on jackknives, scissors, heavy clippers, corkscrews and other lacerating gadgetry I wouldn't know, unless for purposes of slashing his own wrists with a fine expensive blade if conditions get too tough.

It was now two-thirty and I still hadn't found an empty chair. I wondered if there mightn't be some way in which human beings could lock their joints and go to sleep standing up, the way horses do. There isn't. I tried it and the outcome hurtled me across the lobby and up against a desk where Travel Insurance was sold. The girl watched my lurching arrival with fascination. Reassembling my dignity, I pretended I meant to be there right along and took out one of those $2.25 policies whereby my loved ones would be $64,000 to the good in the event of my crashing demise. This fiery possibility always seems to me a certainty whenever I travel by air. It was interesting to note that right next door was a flower shop and I toyed with the idea of also ordering my own funeral wreath in advance. To fill out the insurance form, I leaned on the desk. It was pleasantly restful. So much so, I went on from there in search not of the unfindable place in which to sit but of further objects on which to lean. Western Union has a nice comfortable leaning shelf but I could think of only one wire to send, and Perera Brothers' money exchange has a lovely double-decked arrangement which ought to be just the ticket for resting both arms and, if need be, the head, but I had no immediate use for foreign exchange, even going to Hollywood. I noted some likely looking railings over by the entry for incoming transatlantic passengers. A Scandinavian flight had recently arrived and a crowd was waiting about to meet its occupants. I pushed my way through to a railing and lolled on it for a time, trying to look as though I too had come to meet my cousin Sven from Stockholm.

There are limits to lolling on a railing, so after a while I said to hell with cousin Sven and once more took up my fruitless vagrancy. By

way of sorry entertainment I started counting
the seats provided for the public in this our
nation's leading airport. Right there at the extreme eastern end where hundreds of persons
hang around for hours awaiting the release of
friends and relatives from the prolonged ministrations of the United States Customs there
is resting place for exactly fifteen unless, at the
risk of missing whomever one has come to meet,
one ventures around the corner where are to
be found generous accommodations for twelve.
In the next most populated portion, namely the
main entrance, are some nicely upholstered set-
tees and they also can take care of twelve. There
is, to be sure, one open foyer in the middle of
which are sitting arrangements for thirty-five.
Here, however, the surrounding walls are solid
with airline counters where are constantly being
checked in numberless flights none of which
carry less than forty patrons, and when some of
those flights are delayed, there is no place for the
overflow of patrons to sit unless on the laps of the
previously seated. Two other places, one with
thirty-six seats, the other twenty-nine, are also in
areas frequented by ten times that many people.
The rest are scattered in generous allotments
ranging from six to fourteen throughout the

length and breadth of our mighty air terminal. (I retract the word breadth, for in the quonset hut confines of these cramped purlieus, that dimension is negligible.) All told, I counted two hundred and forty seats. Or rather, two hundred and forty sitters. This may sound like quite a lot. It would be nothing compared with the number of wanderers looking for free seats had I been able to count them too.

I have made some inquiries and find that on an average day about twenty thousand passengers and visitors pass through the portals of Idlewild, to say nothing of the countless employees. When the weather comes down with one of those interesting conditions, these same human beings are neither coming nor going and what most of the poor wretches would like to be doing is to be sitting down. I understand that a new terminal is to be erected. In fact, there's a signboard beside the approaching highway proclaiming the good news and displaying a very tasty picture of the project. The sign also states that it will be some time before the edifice is completed. In the interim, thousands of unfortunates are going to spend thousands of hours in our present shambles wearing themselves to frazzles searching for empty seats. In the interests of humanity, I propose the installation at various points throughout the building of places where one can rent the sort of folding campstools that are to be had on ferry and excursion boats. And in less altruistic interests I'd like here and now to put in first bid for the concession.

. . . I hate zippers . . .

My
Quaking
Hands

I have just been spending an hour of frenzy, frustration and filth trying unsuccessfully to put a new ribbon into a typewriter. Mine is a small, foreign-make portable. It weighs next to nothing, which means that it has a giddy way of moving like an overactivated ouija-board marker about the surface of desk or table when inspiration is burning and words are being pounded out with alacrity and inaccuracy. Any expert typist would drop my modest little machine into the nearest ashcan. In fact, my secretary believes that I keep it by way of penance for some secret fall from grace which she hopes some day to hear about. I am a terrible typist and, as mine is a terrible machine, we get along very well together . . . that is, until the time comes for changing its ribbon. I am able to cope with the spools on either side. I can even stave off those unaccountable knots into which typewriter ribbons will suddenly writhe themselves. What stymies me is that nasty little gimmick in the middle, a Chinese puzzle of slots and crochet hooks . . . all completely ungetatable, even after resorting to tweezers, a hairpin and the use of an elbow to hold up the contraption long enough to thread it. My struggle has ended, as always, in defeat, fury and an appearance of having spent all day being fingerprinted.

I ought to realize by now that changing a typewriter ribbon is one of the things requiring delicacy of touch which I should never attempt. For I am the victim of shaky hands. In fact mine, at times and under specific conditions of stress, are spectacular in their shakiness. For years I went to great lengths to conceal this detriment to my poise and charm. But now since modern psychiatry advises us to admit, if not actually to flaunt our disabilities with a "Hey, look at my tic!" bravura, I might as well come clean and state that there are moments when I am no more capable of opening a softboiled egg than I am capable of performing a brain operation. This is especially true if anyone is watching me, and anyone who happens to be in the vicinity while I am going through the throes of tapping open a piping hot egg without pulverizing the shell or gooing the yolk all over cup, saucer and spoon could not possibly refrain *from* watching me.

Being watched is very trying for the manually tremulous. How many times, in a beauty parlor, have I become uncomfortably aware of the reflection in the mirror of the speculative eye of the lady under the dryer across the way, who has momentarily foregone the delights of her screen-and-TV magazine for the more fascinating sight of my hands fluttering like hysterical bats in a hassle with combs, bobby pins, invisibles and wild wisps of newly washed hair.

Heavy chores, involving muscular effort I can perform with comparative efficiency, if with no particular beauty of motion. It is the manipulation of the small, the lightweight or the delicately intricate that befuddles me into jig-

gling inefficiency. Maybe the most suitable period for me to have lived would have been the
Iron Age. Or perhaps the Stone one.

There are, to be sure, days when my hands
are fairly steady . . . when I can accomplish
actions such as applying mascara to my eyelashes
without applying it also to my cheek, or effect-
ing a nail-polish job which doesn't extend down
over my first knuckle, or . . . and this is most
remarkable . . . threading a needle without
turning it into a hypodermic for my thumb. But
these days of tranquillity are the exception. When
my son was little, his eye had a habit of attracting
cinders, gnats, motes and other oddments with the
accuracy of a magnet attracting steel filings. That
he would run to me for first aid was gratifying to
a mother's heart, but the gesture, if sweetly filial,
was misguided. Concern over the child's predica-
ment would start off my vibrations and my problem was how to remove the foreign body without
also removing the eye. Somehow things would
manage to work out . . . or work the foreign body
out, for my bungling ministrations would fill the
small boy with a terror which in turn filled the
afflicted eye with floods of tears and nature did
the rest. Today, anyone in my household who
catches something in the eye has the good sense

to go ask the corner druggist to perform the extraction. Early in our married life, my husband also had the good sense to give up asking me to help with the studs of his evening shirt. He said that the nervous strain of figuring out how many times I would jab wide of the mark before landing the stud end in its hole mitigated the satisfactions of wifely attention, and besides, the thumbprints I left on the immaculate boiled front didn't look so good.

Over the years I have grown more and more foxy about sidestepping shake producers. Take hot bouillon, for a standard example. Well, actually I never take hot bouillon . . . especially on occasions of stiff formality. The danger lies not in the hot bouillon, but in the small spoon which, after being filled and its adhering drop scooped off on the rim, by the time it trembles up to the mouth contains not one gram of hot bouillon. Cold soup is another matter. One can always defy Emily Post and drink it straight from the cup, which having two handles offers no difficulty. Then there are zippers. I wish there weren't. I hate zippers, but mine is apparently nothing in comparison to the hatred zippers have for me. A zipper, the moment it realizes that it is I who am zipping it, will jam.

Then I get infuriated and yank and the zipper
becomes indignant and jams all the more stub-
bornly and the result makes me realize that I
need never purchase a vibrating machine . . .
my hands can do it all for me. Last month I
acquired a large and rather handsome handbag,
the latest product of a well-known leathergoods
firm who say of it in engraved announcements,
"We are immensely proud of our smart new
town-and-country travel pouch." I am even more
immensely proud of myself for having mastered
the seven separate zippered openings of its
seven separate pockets and compartments. It is a
mastery which has come only after numerous and
humiliating moments of desperate zipper-yank-
ing, bag-plunging (often with bag braced on knee
and knee held waveringly up toward chin) and
further middle-aged gyrations, always during
times of hurry, usually with an indignant line-
up behind me, or an impatient taxi driver waiting with outstreched palm for his fare and holding up traffic while I scrabble for billfold, rail or
plane tickets or the ever elusive pair of reading
glasses.

It is always solacing to encounter a fellow sufferer and I have more than once toyed with the
idea of forming a nationwide fraternity of the

shaky-handed. We could publish an occasional cheery little brochure containing helpful hints, on the order of Alcoholics Anonymous.

And mention of that benevolent organization makes me realize it is time for me to assure any reader who might make the uncharitable assumption that my manual instability is due to alcoholic intake, that such is not the case. For even in my extreme and temperate youth I suffered from the embarrassing affliction. When I attended Camp Gitchee-Goomy, or a name to that effect, my little tentmates gave me the endearing nickname of "Aspen." This was an outcome of my detestation for raffia work. Impatience to get through the tedious hour affected my small digits and the dinner mats I wove to take home as a present for my mother brought forth jeers from my comrades and from the "native crafts counselor" the mark of "Worst in the class." Mother, when presented with the mats, refrained from unkind comment. She also refrained from ever using the mats.

It was later, during my teens, that my unsteady hands became a serious disadvantage. At that period of clear-eyed youth I wanted to be a "Vamp." My ideal was a combination of Theda Bara, Gloria Swanson and a B. F. Keith star named Valeska Suratt who wore a spit curl coiling down from a gold headband and looked mysteriously sultry. I dressed the part within the limits of my schoolbooks-and-soda-fountain allowance, complete with the spit curl, long black earrings from Woolworth's and tears of dismay from Mother. My ambition was ultimately to snare John Barrymore, or failing him, I'd settle for Rudolph Valentino, if not Francis X. Bushman. Until that dazzling fulfillment, I had to resign myself to a negligible assortment of callow admirers . . . Penn State freshmen, Hill School seniors and one pimply visionary who was attending a theological seminary. We called them "men" in those happy Scott Fitzgerald days and "THE thing" was to persuade your "man" to take you to an afternoon *thé dansant* at either the Plaza or a snappy little rendezvous known as the Club de Vingt. One twirled for a while to the intoxicating strains of "I left my love in Avalon," then returned to a pink-lampshaded table for the further intoxicant of significant glances over the rim of a fragile cup of tea. Only I never dared go in for tea. Especially when sipped from a fragile cup. And even more especially as I was usually in love . . . and love was another thing that made my hands shake (it still does). I played safe with a hefty glass of lemonade weighted down with ice and floating globs of fruit, and it is to be doubted if my glances as seen through a thicket of mint sprigs and drinking straws conveyed much significance.

For I had learned the scalding lesson that the full cup could be my undoing. It had already been the undoing of two lace tea covers and the front of more than one frock. All tremble-handers know that between the saucer and the lip, there comes a wobble point as inevitable as anything indicated by the Geiger counter. And when in addition to being full of liquid, the cup is also light of weight, things can be very awful indeed. When I was twenty-one or so, I had a beau whose intentions I fondly believed to be both honorable and serious. Particularly so when he invited me to his house to dine with his parents, persons of quiet dignity and culture. Needless to say that I was nervous. I managed, however, to get through dinner without any mishaps. I had even, before the meal, been able to hold a canapé in one hand and, with the other, toss off a cocktail without slopping anything onto my lap. My downfall was the demitasse. It was also the eventual downfall

of the demitasse which I mistook to be gold
and heavy and instead it was lacquer and feather-
weight, and any prospects of regarding the distinguished couple as potential in-laws was
dimmed by the sight of my tiny cup and saucer
hurtling through space and landing at their astonished feet in the pearl-gray portion of a price-
less Aubusson.

When it comes to my professional life, my
hands have been a real liability. This is doubly
so just before an opening when the first-night
audience is assembling . . . which means they're
still yakking out in the crowded lobby and the
gentlemen of the press are making ready with
their barbed ball-points. On these horrendous
occasions, it's a wonder I am able to get on my
make-up. Indeed, there have been evenings when
it seemed that the only means of attaching my arti-
ficial eyelashes would be to lay the strip on the
dressing table and lower my eyelid down onto it.

Then there are the dangers of stage "business."
I've come to the conclusion that playwrights,
when they become stymied in regard to plot
action or mood, take time out by having their
characters knock off for a drink . . . alcoholic or
otherwise. It has been my fate to have appeared
mostly in the otherwise type of drama. In Lillian

Hellman's *The Searching Wind* I played a dip-
lomat's wife, very suave, very elegant, living
in a suave and elegant Washington mansion.
One scene called for me to pour and serve after-
dinner coffee. Dreading the quake hazard this
entailed, I waited until the probation rehearsal
term was up and I couldn't be fired before con-
fronting Herman Shumlin, the producer-director,
with my problem and asking piteously if please
on opening night would it be possible to have
the demitasse cups glued to their saucers. Mr.
Shumlin, not without logic, made the observation that a small but fashionable group of persons
sipping *espresso* from cups whose saucers were
adhering like sucker fish, would hardly convey
the note of worldly sophistication which the
script demanded.

"Your shakes are all purely psychological,"
said Mr. Shumlin, and he walked away to confer
with others over more vital issues. Sure, I thought,
my shakes *may* all be purely psychological but
just how psychological was it going to seem to
that pair of first-nighters in the front row who
might receive the full impact of a cup and saucer shot into their laps? I took my woes to the
property man, a gentleman of understanding and
deep humanity. He said he'd see. He saw. But

not until just before the opening curtain, at which time he hit upon the device of placing on each saucer a dab of some substance which must have been a combination of honey and Duco cement. It worked fine in so far as the cups, when I handled them, neither rattled nor flew off like clay pigeons. In so far as the rest of the cast was concerned, particularly the other two stars, Dennis King and Dudley Diggs, it gave rise to a certain confusion. When Dennis King raised his cup to his mouth, the saucer came along with it, hit his chin, then plummeted to the floor cloth. Dear Dudley Diggs was so baffled he missed a cue in an absorption of manfully twisting his cup as though unscrewing a bottle top, but never wrenching it free.

I have a close friend who is so sold on psychoanalysis that if she gets a bad case of poison ivy she prefers to spend $25 for an hour on the couch rather than 25¢ for a bottle of calomine lotion. She has often advised me to consult her analyst about my manual palsy. However, before going to such costly and lengthy extremes I decided to consult that fast disappearing and irreplaceable miracle man, the family general practitioner. He performed a number of interesting experiments on my person, hitting my knee joints with a small mallet, staring into my eye pupils with a sharp little light and taking samples of everything except my penmanship. At the end of which exhaustive research he asked me whether or not my father's hands had been tremulous, to which I answered, "And how!" And my mother's? he inquired, and I told him how as a small and cruel child I used to giggle when Mother tried to thread a needle, then added the gratuitous information that my grandfather, who was a clergyman, also had such hand shakes he had trouble turning the pages of the Bible.

"Well, my friend," concluded my honest medic, "all I can say is that you have Congenital Shakes. There is absolutely nothing you can do about them, and I might as well tell you this . . . . the older you get, the worse they'll become."

He was right. They have.

. . . I was younger and more modest . . .

Stage
Fright

A good long while ago, when I was first facing the horrors of an opening night in a leading role, I sought out my father for advice and reassurance . . . of which he gave me what he could. When, however, I asked him despairingly how long one had to be in the theatre before outgrowing stage fright, he looked at me with quizzical compassion and said, "Kiddie" (a term of endearment he used even after I was well on into maturity), "I have been in the theatre for fifty years and I've *never* outgrown it. Any actor who claims he is immune to stage fright is either lying or else he's no actor." And he added further glad tidings: "What's more," he said, "the longer you stay in the theatre, the worse it becomes, because you learn more and you know all the mistakes you can make."

The realization that one's betters have gone through similar anguish is consoling, even if such realization doesn't in the least mitigate the anguish. No less triumphant an artist than Sarah Bernhardt, on overhearing a pert little ingenue boasting of not knowing what *le traque* (stage fright) was even like, is said to have snorted, "Wait until you become a good performer, my girl, and you'll find out." And another French actress, the delicious comedienne Marie Bell, suffered such ghastly and chronic stage fright that she had, literally and physically, to be shoved out from the wings for every first entrance by a sharp clip on her round little rear.

Such occupational panic is not the prerogative solely of people in the theatre. Singers, musicians, all public performers have known stage fright. Lily Pons once told me that every day of of every concert or opera appearance she has

ever given (and happily for the world, she has
given quite a few) she has spent her waking
hours from morn to curtain time being actively
sick at her stomach. Well, at any rate, that's one
way of maintaining a trim and lovely figure.

One takes a certain chill comfort in assuming
that persons of other professions have their cor-
responding heebie-jeebies . . . the lawyer about
to plead a difficult case, the politician faced with
a critical speech . . . even the clergyman, albeit
he has the advantage of divine sponsorship, must
feel an occasional quake of a knee as he mounts
the steps of the pulpit. But not one of these
worthies is as vulnerable as the wretched actor who
has to walk out before an audience and be judged
less, in the long run, by his technical skill than
by his overall personality . . . and then next
day must read the verdict. It's as though some
poor devil were to set out for a large dinner
party with the knowledge that the following morning he would be hearing exactly what each of
the other guests thought about him. Only it's
considerably worse when not just the victim, but
several million readers of newspapers are going
to be reading the verdict. For there is no deny-
ing critics . . . except by the Shuberts who for
a time denied press tickets in any of their

houses to a certain eminently vitriolic one. He, however, purchased his own tickets and continued to write his reviews which were in no wise softened by the reprimand. Toward the end of the seventeenth century, Wycherley while going through the birth pangs of a new play referred to critics as "those vermin of Parnassus" and in case any critics should chance to be glancing over this piece, let me hasten to point out that such was William Wycherley's opinion and not necessarily mine.

Essential as it may be, the presence of these gentlemen of the press (to say nothing of that lady of same out in Chicago) is a definitely contributing factor to stage fright. There are a few actors who claim that they give a better performance under the challenge of knowing that critics are out in front. Well, that's what they claim and far be it from me to question the veracity of a fellow player. I can only record the fact (again an example of misery seeking out comfort) that Sir Henry Irving felt his style to be so cramped by the presence of reviewers, he set down a firm and fast rule that none should attend any opening night, but granted permission for them to filter in for subsequent performances provided that he himself was never to be informed when they were there.

Nice rule if you can make it, but who today commands the power of Sir Henry?

The critics, awesome as they are, are only a portion of that other fright-provoking arbiter . . . that beloved monster, THE AUDIENCE. Again there are actors who will tell you not to think about the audience . . . to ignore them with the lofty attitude that there is not one of them who could step up onto the stage and get away with your part. This advice not only does the quaking actor no damn bit of good, it is highly erroneous reasoning. To pay no attention to an audience would, in my opinion, be to violate one of the principal tenets of acting. For a good performance requires a constant give and take between player and public. It is a sort of ceaseless love affair with all of a love affair's breathless uncertainty, tiptoe sensitivity and eventual delight . . . or despair as the case may prove.

In reality the basic factor of stage fright is not so much fear of the audience . . . not even fear of the critics . . . but fear of oneself. Fear that you won't be able to put on any halfway adequate sort of show. Fear that you'll go completely blank and forget all your lines or that you'll develop an uncontrollable speech impediment. And there are those grotesque

fears . . . the sort Oscar Wilde attributed
to an "imp of incongruity," like thinking you
might suddenly go mad and goose the leading man
or walk calmly up to the footlights and stick out
your tongue at Brooks Atkinson. And a thousand
other goblins; not the least being the one identified by Mr. Roosevelt, the fear of fear itself.

With me, first-night jitters start long before
the zero hour of its rising curtain. Like most
players, I decide to take on a new rôle only if
I am enthusiastically keen to play it, and for
the first weeks after making the decision I'm
all confidence and starry-eyed anticipation. Then
some 3 A.M. when I'm sleeping with the sweet
innocence of those Night-before-Christmas in-
fants, instead of visions of sugarplums dancing
in my head, *plonk!* comes the old familiar shaky-
elevator dream. In this, I am standing on a rick-
ety platform without walls or railing which as it
rises up a dingy shaft wobbles and shudders,
getting farther and farther away from an approaching landing until I stare in horror down a yawn-
ing gap across which, the operator informs me,
I must step or else plunge some twenty stories
to my doom. This fantasy, to the Freudian, will
doubtless be fraught with significance indicative
of unspeakable aspects of my nature, and if it

is, I trust no one enlightens me. I recognize it only as the first of a series of pre-opening dreams. They are indications of the doubts and misgivings which have plagued me ever since at the age of nineteen I waved a fan in the second act of *Blood and Sand* and said, "The bull can't help being a bull, can he?" (my part in its entirety) and they will doubtless continue to do so until I have been admitted to the Actors' Home. Even in those thespian Elysian Fields, if I am obliged to take part in any local theatricals I am sure the same dear old doubts and misgivings will come, cackling along in their wheel chairs. Besides the shaky-elevator incubus, there come those standard nightmares known, I daresay, for centuries to anyone connected with show business. There is the hackneyed one about finding yourself in a strange dressing room, frantically slathering on someone else's make-up while an irate stage manager tells you to hurry, you're late and you ask "What's my part?" to which he answers "I don't know. Just get on the stage," so you ask "What's the play?" but he doesn't know that either . . . at which point you wake trying desperately to say over the lines you memorized the day before . . . and of course you can't remember a single word. There is the further routine dream about trying to get onto the stage and being hindered by innumerable huge obstacles and the one about finally reaching the stage but finding yourself in a semi-paralyzed state when you are either unable to move, or do so with the slow-motion laboriousness of a giant sloth with lead weights on its feet. And there is the lockjaw chimera when you start to say your lines but can't utter a word because your jaws are clenched in a grinding vise which, on waking, you think may have damaged your expensive front-tooth jackets. I used to have a recurrence of that other standby, the whimsy in which, amid a formally attired cast, I walked on stark naked . . . but that was when I was younger and more modest. Now that I am older and more shameless, I don't dream it any more.

As the starting date for rehearsals approaches, the nightmares repeat themselves with increasing frequency until the eve of the initial reading when you dream not at all, because, as a rule, you sleep not at all. This means that next morning with raddled face and halting gait you slink onto the bare stage of an empty theatre to confront for the first time a brand-new cast, crew and director in the white, unshaded glare of the work light. This is an illumination as relentless as that of the morning line-up at police headquarters and one which would reduce the appearance of the prettiest starlet to that of an elderly character woman. You try to assume a charming manner, bare your teeth at everyone in what you hope is a dazzling smile and settle with as much willowy grace as is possible onto a rehearsal chair which is the wooden kitchen variety and often as not has lost its back. You feel that the other members of the company are wondering why the management dug up this old hag for a leading part and you note the speculative eye of your understudy. The reading starts and you have the further feeling that you've completely forgotten how to act . . . if not indeed how to read. But then, here and there, among the circle of readers, you catch a fleeting expression of anguished uncertainty, the nervous clearing of a throat, the rapid trembling of a script . . . and are comforted.

During the weeks of rehearsal, stage fright lets up thanks to hard work and fatigue. And it's not too bad in the interim of road tryouts because of cuts, rewrites, new staging and similar pandemonium. But eventually there looms the prospect of the Broadway opening. Speaking for myself, I think that this mightn't be quite so bad were it not, on the day of a première, for the melancholy behavior of my nearest and dearest. My son has the manner of one who has just learned that his mother is not long for this world, my cook with an expression of acute compassion talks in whispers and tiptoes in with little messes of broth, while my husband spends hours of demonstrable indigestion at his club from whence he keeps calling me with orders to rest and not to talk on the phone. One or two close friends drop by to let me know how nervous *they* are and that I can have no conception of what *they* are going through.

At the end of a hideous day, there comes the walk to the scaffold in the form of a taxi ride to the theatre. In transit I keep praying that we'll have a nice, easy accident . . . the sort that will incapacitate but not hurt, or that New York will be visited by a space ship from Mars and Mayor Wagner will order the closing of all theatres. In my dressing room, where I arrive long before it's necessary, I go through the mechanics of making up, an especially complicated process for me because of my shaky hands. Under this sort of stress they become practically uncontrollable. All the while, of course, I continue my prayers for an honorable way out. Maybe with luck, just after my entrance, I'll be struck down by a falling sandbag, or perhaps I'll be fortunate enough to expire in some less ludicrous fashion, a highly becoming heart attack, for instance. But no such reprieve ever takes place and somehow we live through an opening night as we live through other ensuing ordeals.

For the nasty thing about stage fright is that its attacks are not limited to opening nights. There are times when, for no good reason, it will strike and there is no anticipating these ghastly moments. You may be appearing in a long-run success, assured and cool as a cucumber, when all at once you hear another actor saying his lines and it's as though you were hearing them for the first time and you think, What do I say when he finishes talking? What the hell is my next speech? whereupon you may go into a frozen paralysis from which prompter or fellow player rescues you by throwing you a cue, although mercifully more often habit or the subconcious produces the illusive words which come forth automatically and often in such hollow tones you have the illusion that not you but a complete stranger is saying them. This gehenna of anticipating lines can become epidemic and run through an entire company. During a recent run of *Major Barbara* it was solacing to find out that a seasoned veteran like Charles Laughton came successfully through an attack, and when one evening Eli Wallach went up in a line he knew backwards (and backwards was about the way he said it too) I felt better about the moment when I looked with a wild surmise at Glynis Johns who played my daughter Barbara and couldn't for the life of me think of her name. I, who behind the exterior appearance of a lady am at heart the Wife of Bath, occasionally become the victim of another long-run neurosis, namely the dirty-word phobia, when one realizes that by the mere changing of a letter or two, or the shifting of a simple noun or mild adjective, the most innocent of speeches might be deformed into something censurable in the extreme. The classic example (and just about the only one which can be printed by the dignified house of Houghton Mifflin) was when, on opening night of the revival of Maugham's *The Circle,* an actor whose line, in reference to Lily Langtry, was "Her beauty was such that it took your breath away," came out in clear diction with "Her breath was such that it took your beauty away." I have yet to play a part in which somewhere there is

not the possibility of one of these verbal pit-
falls. The terror of falling into it can become an
obsession. As the sentence involving it approaches
I have found myself breaking into a clammy
sweat. Am I going to say it? Please God don't
let me say it! And even after the line has been
delivered I'll sometimes think, Did I say it? Are
people getting up from their seats and demand-
ing their money back at the box office? But it
is too painful to enumerate more of the actor's
phobias.

What masochistic impulse drives us into this
painful profession? What makes any woman become an actress? What, for that matter, makes
her think she *is* an actress? Such doleful specula-
tion is for psychiatrists and it seems to me I've
already given them plenty to speculate about.
The question arises, Is it worth it? Is the theatrical career worth all the Sturm and Drang?
and the answer . . . again a possible indication
of mental imbalance, is yes. If a show is a hit,
the question never, obviously, arises. Rave reviews and a line-up at the box office can ob-
literate the memory of pain and apprehension
as sweetly as sight of her newborn can oblit-
erate a woman's memories of labor pains. And
if you're in a flop? It's hell . . . miserable,

wretched hell. But the very disappointment and misery seem eventually to rouse a doggedness, a determination to go on and try to make a go of it the next time. I guess what it comes down to is a simple and honest love of one's trade . . . for better for worse, for richer for poorer, in sickness and in health and even for some . . . till death do them part.

55684